This Side
of Tomorrow

ZONDERVAN HEARTH BOOKS

Available from your Christian Bookseller

A HEARTH MYSTERY

This Side of Tomorrow

Ruth Livingston Hill

ZONDERVAN
PUBLISHING HOUSE
OF THE ZONDERVAN CORPORATION | GRAND RAPIDS, MICHIGAN 49506

THIS SIDE OF TOMORROW
Copyright © 1962 by Zondervan Publishing House
Grand Rapids, Michigan

First printing of Zondervan Books
    edition   December 1972

Fourteenth printing January 1981
ISBN 0-310-26062-0

Printed in the United States of America

This Side of Tomorrow

CHAPTER 1

The train sauntered its asthmatic way to another village depot. It was a local the last thirty miles or so before its destination, a little country town whose only reason for existence was the college on a wooded hill.

Sam glanced up from his paperback to read the name on the station. He had glanced up thus at every stop, and each time he had not failed to take another look at the glinting crown of amber hair showing above the dull green of the seat in front of him. Its wide natural wave was like the path of a breeze across a wheat field.

About the three girls on the other side of the aisle, he had little curiosity. Two were mere types, he had decided when he first took his place near them and heard their conversation.

"This year is going to be a blast," declared one in a rapturous strident key. "I'm going to *see* that it is. I spent too much time on books last winter; I don't plan to do that again. Eat, drink and be merry, I say. I've stashed away a fair rating with the profs and I don't intend to worry any more." The girl got out a little gilt-edged comb and mirror and worked with long, slender, practiced fingers on her ash brown slinky hair.

Her seatmate gave her a superior look.

"Have it your way, Pinky, I *do* intend to," she retorted. She was slim, long-legged and long-eyelashed, with sandalwood hair combed back slickly into a twist. Gray green eyes gave her a sort of mermaid mystery look. Her thin shoulders and faintly-lined eyebrows emphasized her words in the proper places. "I'm going to *top* the dean's list this year. I'm looking ahead."

5

"Natch, Brain!" The third girl, an attractive brunette sitting opposite in a reversed seat, broke in languidly with the merest tinge of sarcasm. "No doubt you'll end up with a *Maggie come lousy*. Of course, your last name *is* Wittig. Could Dean Wittig possibly have anything to do with it?"

Edda Wittig caught the barb; her gray green eyes neither winced nor wavered. "I can make it without my uncle," she replied coolly.

Although he had not seemed to cast so much as a flicker of a glance their way, Sam was fully aware that the deep blue eyes of the third girl, facing him, had kept close surveillance upon his every move since he came into the train. All three girls were sophomores, he guessed. How disappointed they would be to discover his freshman status. He was nearly twenty and knew that he showed it.

The train picked up its skirts wearily and began to trudge on, gradually erasing the chatter from Sam's consciousness until the next stop. The rapturous girl was absorbed in a college bulletin of some sort, he gathered, which gave a list of students. She attempted a smart remark over every name, then supplied her own giggle if the others did not laugh.

"John Milton, Lancaster, Pa. He must be a poet. Joan, do you suppose Milton ever dated? Wouldn't it be cool to have a guy bring you a sonnet instead of a corsage? Let's see, Henry Norton, Wilkesbarre. My brother knows him. He's real neat. Oh, my word! Here's one. What some parents do to their children — Wilfred Archibald-Jones Tinker. Wow!"

"Sounds like an in-law to Princess Margaret," quipped Joan Denison, the brunette.

"Oh, but that one's nothing, simply *nothing* compared to this. Just listen! Verna Mae Schiffelgruber!" She deliberately emphasized the incongruous syllables. "Horrors! *What* must she look like? Honestly, this college is getting so many country Dutch it's pitiful."

6

"How right you are," agreed Edda scornfully. "I told my uncle I'd almost rather go to college in New York with the kikes than have to compete here with dumb Dutch!"

Suddenly Sam became aware that something had happened in the seat ahead of him. The figure sitting there had scarcely moved thus far. This was not a movement now; it was not a stir; but there was an unmistakable quivering of the gorgeous amber waves. And as the thoughtless chatter continued, the girl's head turned toward the window. For the first time Sam caught the line of her cheek and temple, where the hair was meticulously combed away from the smooth forehead. Trouble showed in her brow, and as he watched with growing concern, he saw her winking fast; her amber lashes glistened and at last a tear rolled out and had to be hastily mopped away.

The train started on and drowned the conversation once more, but Sam's attention was permanently drawn away from his book. The next stop was their last; the porter had started down the car, taking bags from the overhead racks to place at the exit in readiness. He set some in the aisle while he carried the rest. Sam glanced at the cheap suitcase he had handed down from the amber girl's rack. There beneath the handle were the initials: V M S.

"Hmm!" he thought to himself. "No wonder. Freshman, probably, too. Tough for her."

He tried to get back to his book, but those struggling amber lashes came between him and the page. The train slowed and gave a final sigh. Six slender perfectly groomed legs across the way untangled themselves ostentatiously and made their way to the end of the car. The girls cast disappointed glances at the trim, well built, black-eyed male who had remained so studiously aloof. He did not stir until they were gone. Pinky the giggler, especially, had hoped that he would turn out to be a fellow student.

7

The porter never did return for the last two or three pieces; nor did the solitary girl make a move to leave the train. Sam arose, grasped his own baggage, and reached for the suitcase marked V M S.

The amber eyes looked up, startled. He saw that they were large and troubled, that their owner was very young, most certainly no more than a freshman, and that she had a fresh clean pink and white look although she had obviously done nothing either to subdue or improve it. Farm country was written all over her clean strong hands with their blunt nails, and her sensible, brown, four-eyelet shoes. Sam noted that in spite of the homemade look of her dress, it was of a golden brown that caught the amber shimmer of her hair and set it off to perfection, but, as it were, unconsciously.

"Well, what are we waiting for?" He addressed her pleasantly. "You *are* getting out here, aren't you? It's the college, you know," he added, as she made no move to rise.

"Oh." She hesitated, dismayed. "I — have decided to — go on." She spoke primly, trying to sound mature.

"Go on?" He raised an inquiring eyebrow. "This is the end of the line.

She gazed up at him unbelievingly, a sort of dread in her eyes.

"Well, then I guess I'll have to get out."

"Here, let me take your bag," he offered.

She rose and followed him to the end of the car. Automatically he started to put out a hand to help her down the steps; then he thought better of it. She was extremely tense and nervous as an unbroken colt.

When they finally reached the platform, the last of the arriving students were scurrying to the college bus. They jammed inside, without a glance back to see if there were more, and the vehicle lumbered away up the steep grade toward the stone towers half screened by yellowing maples.

Sam hid his own exasperation; he had a feeling that the girl was momentarily relieved.

"Well, that's that!" he shrugged good-naturedly. "That bus won't be back to make another trip up the hill until five thirty, when the express gets in. We could go over to the drug store on the corner and get something cool to drink," he suggested.

"Oh no! No, thank you," protested the girl hastily. "That is, you go. I'll be all right, right here waiting in the station."

He frowned, then grinned at her. "Say, kid," he chuckled, "you aren't by any chance afraid of me, are you?"

She turned wide amber eyes up to his. "Oh, no sir. Not of *you*." Even in her embarrassment she couldn't help noticing how crisply his hair waved. It was sparkling black, and iridescent as the wing of a grackle in her father's apple tree. "No, not at all. You have been very kind. Just like — " she caught herself.

"Like — ?" he urged with a twinkle. "Don't keep me wondering. And *don't* call me 'sir.' Name's Sam."

"Well, I was going to say like a brother, but my brothers aren't always so thoughtful." She was as serious as a grandmother.

He suppressed an amused smile and wondered what he should do next. Left to himself, he would have sauntered over to the drug store, ordered a sundae, and got out his paperback. But he couldn't get away from the feeling that this girl needed help. He was pretty sure that he knew how she felt.

"How about setting our stuff down over there and we'll rest on that bench under the maple tree and get acquainted?" he offered. "After all, I'm practically sure you are going to be a freshman up there on the hill, and so am I, so let's not waste time."

The girl brightened. *"You* are — ?" she broke off,

9

embarrassed. Her astonished look told him what she was thinking.

"I am! The truth will out. I'm a humble frosh." He laughed. "You wanted to say that I look old enough to be a prof instead."

Mortified, she shook her head quickly, but he went on.

"I'm a few years behind in getting started," he admitted. "I worked awhile after high school. I was here at summer school for a couple of courses, though, to get broken in. That's how come I know about the buses."

"Oh." The monosyllable seemed to be her standby in conversation.

"May I call you VeeEm?" He gave her a guileless look.

She darted an amazed glance at him and turned violently red.

"Why — how did you — ?"

"Very simple, Dr. Watson. I learned to read, even if I have only been to summer school." He roared with laughter at her astonishment. Then as she caught him looking at her suitcase, again the pink coursed up to her temples and a kind of dread seized her once more.

He sobered. "Look here, kid," he said comfortingly, "you're having a bad case of the jitters about going up the hill there. There will be some tough things to meet, but it's all in starting out with the right frame of mind. For one thing," he went on when he saw that he had her concentrated attention, "you want to know as much as you can of what you're going to meet there. You know, it's not a bad break, after all, that we were left here. It'll give me a chance to brief you on a few things that may help."

"Brief — ?" echoed the girl, puzzled.

"Yeah. Fill you in, you know. Inform, disclose, in-

10

struct. Say! You're going to have to brush up a little on the English language."

"English!" she bridled. "It's just that I never heard 'brief' used as a verb before. I always got A in English. I'm here on the Advanced Placement Program."

"Yes, yes, VeeEm, I'm sure of it," he groaned. "That's just the trouble. You'll have so much to unlearn." Why had he ever started this philanthropic project?

She turned to him and stared. "I don't understand." She shook her head slowly.

"Look, VeeEm, don't you realize that you could be a living doll if you'd work at it? Rub some of the corners off. Don't be so square."

She still looked bewildered.

Patiently he began again. "VeeEm, have you ever heard of slang?"

"Yes, of course, I am familiar with it, but we were never allowed to use such words at home. My mother and father did not approve of it." She seemed to withdraw slightly as if pulling her robes about her.

"Man alive!" he exclaimed. "Where have you been?" He looked her point-blank in the face. She colored again and the hurt, distressed look came into her eyes. "Oh, I'm sorry!" he instantly apologized. "I know how you feel. I'm not laughing at you. Honest."

Solemnly she nodded. "It's all right," she said. "I have a lot to learn, I'm sure. You see, we have always lived away out in the country. I went to a very small school and I was never allowed to spend anytime with the rest anyway. But," she added quickly, "I had good teachers, I know, for I made a very high score on my college board test." She was far from boasting; she was simply making a desperate attempt to defend all that she had ever known, all that had made up her life. "But in learning I shall have to be very careful not to lose my standards." Her mouth was a neat little coin purse now, tightly reluctant to give up its

11

thin dime. "You see, I know the Bible very well. We're — that is, my folks are — well, there are lots of things that other people do that we don't think are right." She finished with her back straight and her chin reaching higher and higher.

Sam shrugged. "Well, could be," he said. "I can go along with something like that. But if you are going to live among people you have to talk their language, don't you? However, that's neither here nor there. Let me go over what you'll have to do tomorrow."

"Yes, tomorrow!" she breathed, and her mouth drooped once more. "That's the day I've looked forward to for four years. And now I dread it."

He looked at her squarely. "VeeEm, tell me *why* you dread it."

She turned away, one strong capable hand gripping the other. She opened her mouth but no words came. Finally she cast a despairing look at him and the tears gushed out again.

"Oh, come now, I didn't tell you to cry. I told you to let me in on this thing — tell me all about it. Just pretend I'm your psychiatrist."

She stopped crying and looked startled. "I don't go to psychiatrists." Her prim manner had seized her again.

"Oh, skip it!" retorted Sam. "I mean just come out with the whole story. What's the matter? That's plain English, isn't it?"

But another sob overtook her and she could only blot at her eyes and struggle.

"Well, if you won't tell me, I'll tell you," announced Sam in a matter-of-fact voice, after she grew quieter. "You're upset because those female brats on the train made fun of your name, aren't you!"

"How did you know!" she blubbered. "But it isn't just that. I suppose my name does sound strange to them. They're so different from what I expected. I have looked forward to college for so long. And I

12

thought everyone would be pleasant, that at last there would be a lot of really nice interesting girls to be friends with. But it's not like that. I don't want to go. I know I'm not like the rest. I don't dress like them or talk like them, or even think like them. To them I'll always be 'country Dutch'."

He looked at her soberly for a long time. She thought he was going to scold her. But she was surprised when he said at last in a low husky voice, "I know. How well I know!"

He raised his eyes to hers then, and her sorrows suddenly faded like a wisp of mist. A long moment he read the sympathy and the question in her face before he answered, "I am Jewish."

There was no self-pity in his tone; on the contrary, there was even pride.

Verna said nothing. She was familiar with anti-Semitism, although in her home town there lived only one old Jew, a shoe repairer, and his family. Once she had brought home a report of how pretty and how smart his daughter was; had asked permission to accept the girl's invitation there to dinner, but with one accord the family had all exclaimed in horror, "Chews! You ask to eat yet with CHEWS?" Never again had she mentioned them.

Sam was speaking again.

"I saw my little sister carried home unconscious when she was only five. She had been stoned in the back of her head by neighborhood kids; rotten egg was dripping from her face into her open mouth."

His head was down and his voice was so low she could scarcely catch the words.

"Oh-h!" she gasped. He glanced up and saw in her eyes a sharing of that baptism of pain, a recognition that they were both outcasts together, beyond the pale.

It was only moments that the fellowship lasted. Beside him, Verna felt like a child.

13

Suddenly he sprang up, seized her hand, and pulled her to her feet.

"Well, VeeEm, the first class is over. There comes the express, and here is the bus. Let's go." Then he stopped a moment and gave her a thoughtful look again. "Get rid of those square corners, kid."

Regretfully she followed him. The dread was still there. Dared she trust this handsome stranger? All of her upbringing said no. But something told her he had met a similar problem and conquered. What was right? She shuddered as she climbed into the bus.

If she had expected to travel under Sam's protecting shadow, she was disappointed. Several fellows who had arrived on the express from Harrisburg greeted him, and instead of introducing them to her he paid not the slightest attention to her all the way up the hill. She was relieved, in a way, not to have to converse with all those strangers, but she was hurt, too. He had seemed to be her friend. She wanted to pout. But there was no one to pout to. No one on the bus was even aware of her existence. Everyone was talking fast and renewing old friendships. She tried to tell herself that soon she, too, would know some of these young people, just as her school teacher had pictured to her. But she knew that if it depended on her she would never in this world get up the courage to speak a word to one of them.

A terrible trembling seized her stomach when the buildings loomed in sight and she realized that she was to be let out at one of them alone, to find her own way around and discover where she was to live. Sam did not even rise to carry her suitcase out for her when she alighted. He was laughing with the fellows on the back seat.

The bus had discarded her in front of a big red brick building. Its name was carved over the doorway: Holley Hall. Girls were coming and going. Everyone seemed so sure of themselves. She struggled up to

14

the front door with her baggage, and looked for a doorbell or a knocker. There was none, and all the rest were milling in and out, so she ventured in.

A harassed, secretary sort of person was seated at a desk near the door writing on cards. She glanced up when she saw Verna's shadow nearby, reached her a card and said, "Print your name here, please," and went on writing.

Verna's hand trembled when she returned the card. Would this woman laugh when she read the name? Or snicker? Or even try to hide her amusement? That would be the worst. But she did none of those. She only said woodenly, "Go down the corridor to the left and take the stairway at the end of the hall. Your room will be 305. That's on the third floor. Your house mother's name is Mrs. Ross. She will answer any questions you may have. Supper will be in the main dining room at six. Here is your instruction sheet for tomorrow's registration."

Other girls came crowding in and Verna started down the corridor. It was not that her suitcase was too heavy; she had carried many a heavier load long distances on her father's farm and thought nothing of it. It was her heart that was heavy. What would she find upstairs? She forced herself to push on.

Up one staircase, then up another; all around her the air buzzed with gay chatter, reunions, and squeals of delight. In her bitter isolation she trudged until she found the number 305.

She pushed open the door and peered in. There were two maple beds, two maple dressers and two maple desks, each pair identical. Each desk had a straight chair shoved up to it. There was one comfortable-looking arm chair, and in it, polishing away at her long tapered nails, was Edda Wittig.

CHAPTER 2

The question had been a matter of discussion for years by the whole Schiffelgruber family: should Verna Mae go to college, or should she not?

She herself had thrown the glove into the ring in her first year of high school, after her beloved English teacher had fairly papered the walls of the girl's imagination with scenes of the opportunities which higher education could offer.

It was at dinner one evening. Mr. Schiffelgruber at the head of the table was hunched over his soup bowl, spooning up the thick bean and bacon mixture in regular even rotation, like a conveyor. After every three spoonfuls his lower lip reached up with a vehement sucking sound to cover the ends of his long graying mustache, to retrieve from it any clinging bits of nourishment that might otherwise be wasted. A Schiffelgruber considered wastefulness a sin. Gramma Schiffelgruber, his mother, sat at his right, her crutch hooked conveniently over a protruding nodule on her chair back. Her glasses, resting low on the bridge of her large nose, were thick lensed, and she seemed to examine every slow spoonful before she placed it in her mouth.

Next to her was Richard, nearly three, born embarrassingly late after the family was supposed to have been complete. He adored his grandmother and his one sister, Verna Mae, seated on his other side, possibly because they were the only ones who had never given his little subconscious the feeling that he should not have come.

Mrs. Schiffelgruber sat at the opposite end of the table from her husband. She had long ago suggested that his mother should have that place, and she would gladly sit at one side, but a family conclave decided that the other arrangement was more scriptural, though chapter and verse for the decision were quite vague.

Mrs. Schiffelgruber was tall, with long, sunken cheeks and a tight small mouth. Her hair had once held some of the amber that glinted in her daughter's now, but hers had long since faded to drab. It still showed a daring tendency to wave, however, on damp days. Mrs. Schiffelgruber was a most dutiful wife in every way but one; there were times when she felt she *must* have flowers in the house, and once she had even ventured to tuck a jaunty yellow daffodil in her hair. But she forgot to remove it before her husband came in for dinner and she never did it again.

On the other side of the table were ranged the four grown sons, according to their age, from the eldest to the least, who was fifteen but already strong enough to do a man's work on the farm.

The rest were nearly finished with their dinner when Verna Mae had everything served and sat down with them.

"Father," she began in a hollow yet determined tone that drew everyone's attention, "I want to go to college when I finish high school."

Mr. Schiffelgruber dropped his spoon with a clatter, sucked his mustache and stared at her.

"College!" he exploded. "That's the last place I want a daughter of mine to go."

Verna Mae stood her ground. This was no more than she had expected. "Why not?" she asked in a steady voice.

"Why not? Money is why not. Worldliness is why not. Wickedness in high places is why not. What do you want to go to college for?"

"So that we can *have* things and *do* things like other people. Every time I want something, it's either wrong or we can't afford it." She spoke hotly. "My teacher

17

says that I'd be able to make twice as much money. I can give you statistics. If my brothers had a college education they would be able to hold really fine positions."

"What's the matter with what your brothers are doin' now, I'd like to know?" stormed the father. "There's nothin' better than working the ground yet. That's the only thing the good Lord told Adam to do in the beginning, to till the ground. If man hadda kep' to that he wouldn't get into such a peck o' trouble all the time. An' as fer bein' like other folks, look at Israel. They wanted a king like other nations, an' what happened? They fell into *sin* like other nations, and God *gave them up*. Don't talk college any more to me." Mr. Schiffelgruber shoved his chair back noisily, left it where it was, and stalked out of the room picking his teeth.

Verna Mae set her chin a little more firmly and went on to finish her dinner. The rest were soon done and everyone left the table except her grandmother.

"Don't try it, VernaMae," she advised softly. The family always spoke the girl's name as if it were one word.

"I've got to, Grandmother!" The girl had chosen to call her father's mother by the longer word instead of "Gramma" ever since she had heard her English teacher speak lovingly of her own grandmother. No teasing by the others could move her.

"You don't understand, child. You know you've been brought up to be a good Christian girl, ain't?" She went on as Verna nodded. "Well, you don't want to go back on all you been taught, do you?"

"No, but Grandmother — "

"Don't interrupt, VernaMae. I've lived a long time an' seen a lot. There's more sin than there needs to be because young folks has gone off to college and give up all they've learned at home. No, the Lord won't bless you." She shook her head, peering over her

18

glasses. Her granddaughter wondered if everyone's ears grew so large when they were old.

"Why, VernaMae, you was always the best little Christian even when you was a tiny thing. You always went to church without fussing, an' you learned to say your verses so pretty, and sang your little songs, right on key, good and loud. An' even now, you're singing in the church choir, and I'd like to know who's called on to pray oftener 'n you in the young people's meetin's. No, you got a good start, VernaMae, an' you mustn't go back on it."

"I don't intend to go back on anything, Grand-mother."

"But you will! You can't tell me diffrunt. I seen 'em, over an' over again. Each one argues that he won't be changed but they all are."

Verna Mae was silent, but she had not given up. When she discovered that it was possible with high grades to earn a scholarship to the state college, she worked feverishly up to the head of her class. Every time she discovered an argument which might carry weight with her family she planned carefully how to bring it out to best advantage. Toward the end of her senior year, when the scholarship money was practically assured, she began to realize exultantly that opposition was breaking down. Her brothers were her strongest allies. One of them even gave her ten dollars toward her expenses. And the day that her mother came home with a suitcase with her initials on it she knew that she had won.

She threw her arms around her mother's neck and sobbed for joy.

Mrs. Schiffelgruber was not used to such emotion and she tried to pass it off.

"They was sellin' cheap," she explained, "because they was shopworn. An' the store put on the initials for nothin', so your father figured it was a real bargain an' I couldn't turn it down."

The few friends Verna Mae knew at school and at the little country church were openly envious; some were jealous to the point of bitterness. The whole family of Schiffelgruber was criticized in some quarters. But in general the folk who lived round about wished her well.

"We'll pray you through, VernaMae," promised her minister, patting her shoulder. "Don't you lose your religion. Compromise is of the devil. It's an evil world you're goin' into," he warned her lugubriously. Then he added piously, his voice rising higher, only to fall on the last two syllables, "but the angel of the Lord will protect you."

Verna Mae appreciated his encouragement; at least she took for granted that she did. She knew that what he had said was true; she did not doubt his sincerity. She had never doubted a single word of what he preached so energetically every Sunday. But she felt secure in her faith; it was all she had ever known.

The meagre shopping that was permitted by the head of the house in preparation for her departure, was done, not by Verna Mae, but by her father and mother, accompanied by her grandmother. The old lady limped along, managing her crutch with one arm and clutching her enormous Bible with the other. She never stirred anywhere without it.

Not one article was purchased without haggling over the price. Before the ordeal was over the girl wished that she could have gone off with half as many things and no argument. As it was, her wardrobe was pitifully small. But Verna Mae had been brought up to understand that clothes were not the criterion of character, and the latter was all that she should be concerned about. So she tried to quiet various inward misgivings as she made ready to leave.

The night before she left, her mother, in an unwonted burst of emotion, allowed herself to kill two chickens for dinner.

But instead of being a sort of gala occasion, the meal was unusually silent. The chickens turned out to be tough ones, and Mr. Schiffelgruber complained, since he always removed his upper teeth before eating, much to the annoyance of his wife and daughter. The big brothers chewed away noisily; Grandmother ate little, shaking her head at intervals and then closing her eyes and moving her lips as if in prayer.

Mrs. Schiffelgruber insisted that her daughter sit down and be waited on this last night at home, but that only made Verna Mae uncomfortable. Richard, nearly seven now, was the only one who seemed at ease. He kept asking his sister innumerable questions, all of them the wrong ones, which made the atmosphere still more tense.

To add to the uneasiness, the sky was dark with a coming storm. It had been a very hot day for early September; humidity thickened the air. Everyone in the house dreaded the coming of a thunderstorm, for Grandmother always insisted on closing all doors and windows, no matter how sweltering the day had been. She demanded that everyone gather in the dining room, as the place where there was the least likelihood of a draft, and there she would beguile the time by alternating melodramatic prayers with stories of tragic deaths by lightning. They had all heard the same tales over and over, but they were expected to shudder afresh, and many of them did.

Yet not everyone of the family reacted to this stimulus in the same way. Verna Mae had learned to invent all sorts of excuses to slip away to her own room where she would open all the windows and delight in the magnificence of the rolling thunder. She exulted in the sudden thrill of the lightning darts and the fresh dank smell of rain-washed earth. She had read in the Bible that thunder sounded like the voice of God and that lightnings were called His messengers. At such times she watched the mighty powers in the

21

vastness above her and felt a deep longing to know the God of all those wonders. Somehow she felt a little nearer to Him, as if just she and He were out there in the storm together. But the feeling always passed and she would sigh and turn away obediently when one of her brothers was sent to fetch her. *Some* day she would go right into the storm and meet it head on.

But that night the storm clouds died away without their usual refreshing shower. The night remained hot, and sleep was difficult for most of the family.

Verna Mae rose at four, went through her usual routine of chores, and was ready, after the six o'clock breakfast, for her brother to take her to the station at seven. Her father did not come in from the field to bid her good-by, but her mother managed a farewell kiss, and the girl thought she detected a dampness around her eyes. The gaunt woman opened her mouth in a troubled way, but no farewell warning for her daughter was forthcoming. Grandmother, with crutch and Bible, stood somberly in the doorway, shaking her head. With a V in her forehead she whimpered, "Now mind you, VernaMae, and read your Bible every day, will you, VernaMae? Promise you'll say your prayers every night."

"I will," agreed the girl obediently. "Don't you worry, Grandmother," she added confidently. Richard went along in the jalopy and gave his sister a hug and a childish squeeze when the train pulled in.

"Bring me a present when you come back, Verna-Mae," he begged. She returned his hug and hurried away.

There was a two-hour ride, then a long wait during the morning for the westbound train. But when it came, and she settled back in the green plush seat, thinking that at last all was rosy, in came those girls and spoiled the whole picture. It was a grueling day.

Edda Wittig raised her eyes by degrees, taking in the new girl's shoes and cheap suitcase, then the anomalous cut of her dress, and finally her hair, beautiful in itself but too long to be stylish.

"Oh, it's you," she remarked without cordiality. "Well, I hope you like to study. Because I want it quiet here evenings."

The newcomer stood with her eyes fixed on the other girl for a long moment. But she was not looking at her. She was trying to think of a way to get out, to run away. She wanted to fling her suitcase full in the face that had scrutinized her so critically and flee out of this girl's sight forever. She was afraid to speak lest her voice tremble and she give herself away for just what she was, a frightened freshman, and a country Dutch one, at that.

But not one sign of her inward tumult betrayed itself to Edda. The stolid endurance of generations of Teutonic ancestors served to steady her, so much so that Edda mistook it for poise. However, "Just dumb!" she reported to the rest later. "Dumb Dutch. She didn't even know she had been told off. It will take more than that to squelch her." But inwardly Edda was aware that she had not won the first round. At best it was a draw.

At last the freshman spoke. "I like to study." She said it in a calm, even tone, very casually, and came in and set her bag down on the bare desk top. She suddenly remembered her English teacher saying, "It won't *all* be glorious, you know. There will be some rough spots." This was one, she decided, that looked very much as if it would not be a mere spot, but a long road with no end until June.

There was a long silence. Verna tried hard to think of the right thing to say, but no thoughts came. Edda Wittig did not care whether she said the right thing, or anything at all. She made up her mind to see her uncle the very first thing and make him use his influence to shift roommates. It was bad enough for her,

23

as good a student as she was, to have to room with a mere freshman, but such a freshman!

The new girl set about putting her things away. No help was forthcoming to show her which closet was hers, or which dresser. She discovered by trial and error. If she had any preference it would have done her no good. She wanted to ask where things were but she didn't dare. After fifteen or twenty minutes of no communication, Edda arose and left the room.

Verna Mae stood still and looked about her disconsolately. She could imagine Edda rushing into the rooms of those other girls and breaking the terrible news to them, or seeking commiseration. Tears were very near again, but at any moment that disdainful girl might return; she could not afford tears.

At six she made her lonely way to the dining room, following the general direction which the majority of young people were taking. There was a long line, for the meals were served cafeteria style. Third ahead of her was Edda Wittig. She seemed barely aware of the chatter of a group of girls with her; her chin was up in a superior manner, and her gray green eyes were roving constantly about the room as if in search of some spirit more kindred to hers. When her attention came to rest a few moments, unconsciously Verna's eyes sought the object of her interest. It was Sam, seated at a nearby table with two other fellows. He happened to glance up at just that minute, perhaps in subconscious reaction to Edda's stare. His gaze passed over her carelessly and slid down the line. Then he glimpsed Verna, noted her droop of loneliness and flashed a comradely smile. Just an instant it was, but all at once the big dining hall seemed less formidable, and her college year a little less terrifying to Verna. Her answering smile lingered on her lips, shapely when they were not prudishly pursed, and Edda saw it. A fierce contempt spread the delicate line of her nostril and she cast a withering look at her roommate and

24

again at Sam before she turned her seeking eyes back and forth over the assortment of faces once more.

It was Verna's turn at the serving counter now. She passed along the row, feeling that at least she had a right to be here, and she was one with all the rest. How hunger leveled the human race! Then it happened.

Just as she left the rail with her tray full of food someone jostled her arm just enough to upset her glass of iced tea. She tried to save it but in doing so, the whole tray became unbalanced and turned upside down on the floor with a loud messy clatter.

In dismay Verna took one look, then she turned and fled, out of the room, down the stairs, across the campus and up to Holley 305. It promised little comfort, but at least that hateful girl was not there. She flung herself down on the bed near the window and sobbed her heart out.

The more she thought about it, the more certain she was that it had been her roommate who turned away from the water fountain so suddenly as to jostle her. Did she mean to do it?

Verna wept and wept. Darkness came on and there were sounds of girls returning, running, walking, laughing, calling. Soon that girl would be back. She dreaded to meet her.

Her mind rushed here and there, trying to find an open door of escape. Home wouldn't do. Not now, not after all the years of planning and scrimping. New York? Or some other city? It seemed to her harassed thoughts that any other place would be less cruel and unfeeling than this one. She recalled a conversation between her father and mother when the dispute over her college venture had been at its height.

"She don't really want larnin'," he argued. "It's jest that she wants to try her wings," her father had scoffed. "She's jest like Tulip, always wantin' to get her head through the bars, to the next pasture." Verna suddenly had a feeling that she was that cow and, like Jonah and his gourd, she had pity on the cow.

Finally her good Dutch training came to bear on the financial aspect. She had won a scholarship. Was she to throw that to the winds because of a snobbish girl who disliked her? She sat up and mopped her eyes.

"All right," she said aloud, "I'll live with her if I have to, but I'll get better marks than she does."

Just then there came a knock on the door.

CHAPTER 3

The Goldmans were a close knit family. They had to be and they loved to be. When the children were small they had lived in a tiny row house on a not too desirable street. Mrs. Goldman kept it immaculate, but in spite of that, Harry and Sam, coming home from school, and even little Rose in her playpen in the wee back yard, were accustomed to shouts of "Dirty kike, we no like!" sometimes to the accompaniment of rocks or rotten vegetables retrieved from the gutter. When Rosie was old enough to go to school, Mrs. Goldman finally took to meeting the children halfway home. Something about her calm, dignified bearing put a damper on the hoodlums' more violent expressions of scorn. But this did not always work. Even she had come home with bruises occasionally. But the family stuck doggedly to the cheap neighborhood in order to save, primarily for the children's schooling, and also for another precious project, rarely mentioned.

The inside of the house did not give the impression of penury. Its furnishings were few but they were of good quality and they were artistically arranged. There was a bright hominess about it, too. The few children on the block who were allowed to visit there loved Mama Goldman's honey cakes, distributed freely. They found themselves remembering with pleasure the bright red geranium in the one front window, framed by spotless white ruffled curtains. They didn't know or care that the curtains had been painstakingly darned from time to time through the years. They only sensed that the bright flower seemed noticeably contented to bloom there; perhaps because it was loved. The bar mitzvah parties for Harry and later for Sam were the most fun; then the little house was jammed with all manner of Goldman relatives and friends. The Goldman children would never forget those years.

In those days Mr. Goldman was just a clerk in the book section of the big department store downtown. It was not until Harry had finished high school and was ready to start his premedical training that his father was made head of the book department and was allowed to put into operation his dream of years, a lending library right in the store. Besides his own love for books, Harry Sr. had a double purpose in choosing to work among them. He knew that he could never afford all he wanted for his children to read; but if he had access to a library and the sample copies of new titles sent to buyers, his children would never lack. There was great rejoicing in the Goldman family when the promotion took place. For Father Goldman was the revered and beloved head of the house.

But even when increases in salary tempted the family to move to finer quarters, father and mother took counsel and decided to endure the close quarters another year or two till Harry got through college. Then it was Rose. She had skipped in school and caught up with Sam, graduating at sixteen. They all agreed that Rose, the student, should go straight on to college. Sam, who adored his pretty soft-eyed sister, insisted that he help out. His brother Harry, he said, was too near his degree for him to stop now.

"I'll get more out of college if I work awhile, father," he urged. So he got a job on a local newspaper where there was plenty of leg work and all manner of experiences. After two years Rose was able to earn a working scholarship for her last two years, and now Harry was married and an interne in the city hospital.

So the Goldmans moved to a pleasant roomy house in a suburb far enough in the country to have some space around the house for Mrs. Goldman's long coveted garden. And at last Sam enrolled in college.

But even then the older Goldmans spent many hours lying awake at night discussing for the future.

"We must see to it that there is enough for Rose's wedding," fretted Mama Goldman.

"Ah, but Rose is not yet even engaged, Mother," reminded her husband. "She will be particular about choosing. She has discernment."

"That is another reason why we must have plenty laid by," argued Esther. "She will marry well and she must have a fine wedding."

"It seems only yesterday that she started off to school," sighed her father.

"All the more will tomorrow come quickly." Esther's habit of years was not to be lightly relinquished. "And Sammy will be needing a little help, too, for his first year in college. He has been so unselfish, that Sammy."

"We have good children, Esther," agreed Harry Goldman. His voice grew husky. "We can thank God for them; they are like olive trees. And you are my fruitful vine, my own dear." He drew her close to him. It was not often that Harry allowed even Esther to know how tender was his heart. She clung to him a long moment, revelling in the immaculate oneness of their family. So many families were torn by strife, at cross purposes with one another. But the Goldmans had common ideals; they always understood one another — or at least almost always.

28

Esther gave a long sigh. Harry alerted to it instantly. "What is it, dear?"

"Harry, do you think that Rosie is — is just the same? Is it my imagination that she had something new, something foreign to us in her mind when she was home this summer?"

Harry was silent a long time. Esther waited. He, too, sighed.

"If it is your imagination, it is mine, too," he replied at last.

"Do you think it comes from the college? Has the atheistic teaching she has told us about drawn her away from the God of our fathers?"

"I think not. She discussed very freely with me the theories of all the professors. It is not that. She is sound as a green olive in her faith in Jehovah. But there is an influence somewhere that is changing her."

"Do you think she is in love?"

"She does not act like a girl in love. And she does not single out any man to talk of. Yet all this year she has been different, as if she had something on her mind."

"Perhaps she is worrying over working and trying to keep up her grades this year?"

"Rosie worried over school work? When did she ever have trouble with that? She may be anxious over her new job. It's a big responsibility to help look after all those girls. I'm proud that they chose our Rosie." Harry Sr. sighed again, then changed the subject. "I think Sammy will do well in college. His years on the newspaper have matured him. I wouldn't be surprised to see him outstrip Harry."

They continued far into the night discussing their children's tomorrows.

And invariably at times like these, another subject, hidden deep in their hearts arose to be fingered delicately, wistfully, in almost stealthy tones. "Do you think it might be in our lifetime?" one would always

29

ask. "It might be," the other would agree yearningly. "Sometime it will happen. We shall keep on saving."

That same evening, after dinner, Sam had stopped at a telephone booth in the men's dorm and called his sister Rose, over in Holley Hall.

"Hi, Rosie, I'm here," he greeted her. "Got in just before dinner. Say, I have a job for you. A new girl in your dorm needs a pal. She's scared, and a square, to begin with; and several brats made it tough for her on the train; I heard it all. You know what it's like. Then tonight she had a smashup in the mess hall. Look her up, will you? She'll probably bite your ear off, but you can take it! Name's Schiffelgruber; that's part of her trouble. She's got amber hair; you can't miss her. Okay? Thanks. So long. Be seein' ya."

Rose hung up the receiver and hesitated. Should she hunt up Mrs. Ross, the regular house mother? But this girl probably needed only a cheerful welcome. All the freshmen were nervous at first. She flipped through the card index. Schiffelgruber! No wonder the poor child was teased. What a boy her brother Sam was. Most fellows wouldn't notice or care. He went out of his way to help underdogs. But so did Rose, especially if they were only underpuppies. No wonder she was a sociology major.

When Verna heard the knock, she assumed at first that it was her enemy, returned to harass her. Then she realized that the girl would not knock at her own door. Verna hastily smoothed back her hair, mopped her eyes, and went to the door. She had no idea how woebegone she looked to Rose.

"Oh!" exclaimed Rose. "Did I disturb you? I am just Rose; I help Mrs. Ross. I stopped by to see if you're getting settled all right. Your name is Verna, is that right?"

There was warmth in her tone that was like home hearth fires to the desolate girl. She nodded. She dared not trust her voice yet.

30

"Did you come far today? You're tired, I'll bet. Have you met your roommate yet?"

Verna had started to answer the first question, but at the second she stopped and froze.

"No! — that is, yes." She pursed her lips and stiffened the back of her neck. There was no expression in her tone.

Rose took a long guess. She laid a gentle arm across Verna's shoulders and looked her straight in the face with an engaging smile.

"Don't tell me you and she have had a run-in already!" she said, as if it was nothing unusual for roommates to quarrel frequently. "Or have you goofed somehow? Come on, you're upset, honey. Let me in on it."

Verna started to pull away stiffly, but at the other girl's sympathy suddenly she broke down and sobbed again.

Rose drew her down to the edge of the bed and waited, with her arm around her. She stroked the beautiful amber hair softly. At last Verna got control again and began to stammer an apology.

"Don't mind a bit, honey," Rose soothed. "Lots of freshmen lose their nerve at first. I just about did myself. This your first time away from home?"

Verna nodded.

"You'll get over it. Don't you worry. You'll have a good year and laugh at yourself one of these days."

"Oh, but you don't know what I did!" burst out the freshman. "Someone jostled me and I dropped my whole tray in the dining room. It was terrible! In front of all those people! I'll never be able to face them again. I can't eat there, ever!"

Rose laughed softly. "Honey, you're not the first one that has happened to. Lots of kids have done it. It's no crime."

"Oh, but you don't know how it feels to have everyone look at you and jeer."

31

Rose looked serious, then she said softly, "You won't believe me, but I really do. I'm Jewish! I've had that all my life."

Startled, Verna looked up at her. "Why!" she exclaimed, "you sound like Sam! He was so nice to me today."

A slow smile stole over Rose's face. "I'm glad he was. I'll give him a good mark for that. You see, he's my big brother."

For the first time that day Verna let an uninhibited smile light up her face.

"Of course! Your forehead is just like his! And your hair — that beautiful black like a grackle's wing among apple blossoms! Oh!" Horrified, she clapped her hand over her mouth. Rose laughed a low ripple.

"I won't tell," she promised. "But you are very poetic. You have lovely hair yourself, did you know it?"

"Me? No, I've never been lovely in any way. I don't know how. I've *never* been any good at anything," she burst out again. "Everyone else has friends and nice clothes and they go places and do things."

Noisy voices sounded suddenly in the corridor and Edda pushed the door open.

"Oh, my word!" she spat out disgustedly. "If it isn't the United Nations Council. Well, you can clear out now. I want to go to bed. I'm tired."

Verna started to freeze again but Rose replied graciously, as if she hadn't heard the insult, "Oh, it's Edda Wittig, isn't it? I remember you from last year. It's nice to see so many girls coming back again. Your roommate here will need to be shown the ropes tomorrow, Edda. I'll count on you to help her."

Edda curled her lip. "You can count to a thousand if you like. I've got plenty to do myself. No one ever had to show me the ropes. I made my own way and she can too." Edda had partly undressed and now she began to cream her face.

32

Rose tried to think quickly. It would be cruel to leave a new, frightened freshman in this situation her first night, but if she took her part Edda had it in her to make things ten times worse for Verna. Verna was going to have to meet this herself and learn to conquer it by living with it. The slightest sign of partiality to Verna might give the girl a whole winter of misery. So Rose laughingly started out the door, saying,

"There, Verna, you're on the spot. But you'll make it. We were all freshmen once. See you both in the morning. Good night now."

She closed the door with the feeling that she had thrown a fledgling Daniel to the lions.

Sam had not expressed any choice of roommates on his application blank.

"No, Rosie," he insisted when she had suggested a name or two of fellows she had liked, "I'll take my chances. That way I'll meet new people all the time. I like to. It'll help if I'm going all out for this writing deal."

Since he had not arrived on the early bus from the station, one of the other three occupants of his room had already slung his stuff on beds and desks and departed to explore. But another was standing in front of a chest of drawers meticulously placing a neat pile of clean, initialed handkerchiefs. He looked up with a pleasant smile as Sam came in, trotted over to him and put out his hand.

"I'm Oliver Thnead," he lisped cordially. One of his front teeth was rather too long for the rest; occasionally it caused difficulty in his speech. He was short and slender and wore round rimmed glasses. His shoes were new and shiny, but his handclasp was empty of personality. *As if there was no one inside,* registered Sam, at the same time returning his handshake pleasantly enough, although he had not expected such a formal greeting.

33

"Hi, Snead. Sam Goldman. Any of the others arrived yet?"

"There's baggage here. They must have gone thomewhere," suggested Snead eagerly. He hovered about Sam as if trying to be helpful. "Are you a — thenior?"

Sam chuckled. "No soap. Freshman. I'm just dumb!"

"Oh," responded Oliver, obviously disappointed. "I wondered." Then he added, "Well, tho am I." Sam wondered whether he meant he was a freshman, or dumb. He let it pass.

"Yeah? Where're you from?"

"Thcranton. Just graduated in June. I'm nineteen. I had to repeat tenth grade, heh-heh." He gave an apologetic little shake of his small, drab head. "But I like photography. I take a lot of pictures." He started to get out his camera to show to Sam.

Sam began to wonder whether he had been wise not to ask for a choice of roommates. He was not one to worship brawn, but he towered over the little fellow as much as eight or ten inches; he certainly was not drawn to him at first sight.

"You're a real cat, aren't you?" Oliver looked up at him admiringly.

"Me? Not even doggy." Sam brushed him off like a bit of lint and went out. "I can't take much of that!" he groaned inwardly. He went on down the hall, saw someone he knew, and promptly forgot Oliver Snead.

He met Colley Corbett at lights out time. He was the opposite of Oliver. An enormous chest and arms, a low broad forehead, reddish hair, and a chin like a bulldog. His waist was slim and his legs solid. He was constantly pulling in his abdomen, drawing a little gasping breath as he did. A weight lifter, Sam decided instantly. It turned out that Colley's older brother owned a chain of health studios; he was putting Colley through college, chiefly because he wished that he had more sophistication himself. Colley was anxious only to please his brother.

The last of the quartet would not arrive till morning.

As Sam fell asleep the round amber light from someone's flashlight outside glinted on the copper screen. It reminded him of that girl's amber hair. She sure had beautiful hair. But what a square she was! Poor kid. He wondered whether Rose had found her.

CHAPTER 4

When Rose closed the door Verna felt as if she were shut in with the devil for eternity.

She froze and waited. She could not think of Edda in any other way than as an opponent. That self-possessed young woman, however, proceeded steadily on her course of preparation for a night's rest. She addressed not a word, look or gesture to the trembling freshman. At last Verna took her toothbrush and other necessities and went down the hall, more to escape than to prepare for bed.

When she came back the lights were out. Edda had pre-empted the bed nearest the window, without a by-your-leave. Verna wondered whether she might decide to change when cold weather came.

Silently Verna slid out of her clothes and knelt a moment beside her bed, thankful at least for the shielding darkness. Nightly prayer had been Verna's habit since she could remember and she had been warned repeatedly by her mother and her pastor not to forsake the Lord. It was a question, however, whether she was more conscious of the Divine Presence, or the presence of the hostile girl. At any rate, she went through the accustomed motions with determination.

She slept more for sorrow than for refreshment. The night remained hot.

Morning was still humid. Verna woke early and with a sudden sinking of the heart oriented herself before she opened her eyes. She tried to discern by ear whether Edda was awake or whether she had already left the room. When she detected her steady breathing Verna slitted one eye open toward her. Edda looked much older than she probably was, lying there relaxed, with her hair in a pale green net and her mouth sagging. Verna studied her face. It wore a droop of discontent, even in sleep. *How could any human being be as mean as she?* thought Verna. *So she thinks she's a brilliant student? Whatever she does,* Verna decided fiercely, *I will do it better!*

All at once Edda's eyes opened without warning, and she gazed straight into Verna's staring ones. Resentment flared up, and hate, along with mortification at being caught unawares. She did not speak. Her usually quick mind was at a loss to express her fury at what she considered intrusion on Verna's part. But she needed no words to convey her thoughts. Verna snatched her gaze away and rose. Grabbing her toilet articles, she rushed out of the room to wash. How much longer could this go on? How much worse could it get? Verna washed more than one tear away at the old-fashioned gray and white mottled sink. Other girls were coming and she dared not dawdle too long. Everyone but Verna seemed to be happy and eager. How would she ever get through the long months ahead?

Breakfast presented the immediate ordeal. Maybe if she went early there would be few students there. Perhaps they would not identify her as the awkward blunderer of last night.

But the first person she met just ahead in the line was Edda's friend Joan.

She flung her an uncordial "Hi!" *As if I were a glass of lukewarm water!* whimpered Verna to herself and shrank a little farther within her own ego.

Then a voice with a familiar edge to it sounded almost directly behind her: "Better carry her tray for her, Joanie," jeered Edda.

Verna's cheeks blazed red and her hands trembled so that she was actually in danger of dropping the tray again. She did manage to navigate to the farthest table where she sat down with her back to the rest of the dining room.

She choked down her cereal and attacked her egg. It was cooked the way she hated eggs, neither hard nor soft. She was torn between wanting to stay and toy with her food till the rest were gone and finishing quickly to get out of the room. Her thrifty upbringing would not allow her to waste food that was already paid for by the semester, so she stayed.

She had managed the last unpalatable bite when she heard footsteps behind her. A tray appeared on her table, a chair began to move, and a voice said heartily, "Top of the morning to you, VeeEm. In other words, 'Shalom.'"

Sam sat down smiling.

Again the whole world changed color. It wasn't as hot as it had been; eggs didn't taste half bad cooked like that; even Edda was only another miserable human being.

Verna broke into a really lovely smile, then she colored, suddenly aware that this most desirable young man was going to eat breakfast there at her table, while those other girls watched. She wished he wouldn't. She dreaded the remarks that Edda would make afterwards.

"Well, how is the world treating you this morning?" he began genially. "It isn't as bad here as you feared, is it?" He gulped down a glass of orange juice.

"Oh, sir — I mean Sam," she flushed again and grinned, "it's ever so much worse!"

He raised his fine black brows. "Really? I sent my sister up to get you acquainted last night. Didn't she find you? Rosie could cheer up old Mephisto himself."

"Yes, she came. She's lovely. She looks just like the picture of Queen Esther in a Bible story book I had when I was little. But — "

"But your roommate. Is that it? Who is she?"

Verna spoke in a voice hushed with dread. "That awful girl in the train yesterday!"

"You're kidding! What a deal! Which one? The tall one, I'll bet, with the green mermaid eyes? It would be. Why couldn't it have been that little dark one they called Joan. She looked not half bad." His tone held a measure of admiration. Verna wondered why she resented it. "Well, you'll live through it." He finished his egg and poured down a glass of milk. "Don't let her get you down. Tell her where to get off occasionally. You'll make it. Well, it's about time to go sign up. Call on Rose when you need her. I'll be seein' you," he added, rising and flinging a careless wave of his hand back at Verna. He strode down the length of the room and disappeared.

His coming and going had been so delightful and so unexpected that Verna was still struggling for emotional balance. She made her way slowly out looking neither to right nor left, lest she happen to meet the baleful gaze she had learned to dread.

The morning consisted of waiting in long lines. Sometimes a girl or one of the fellows standing next in line would try to open a conversation with her or make some casual passing remark. Verna was always so obviously embarrassed that they soon turned away. Altogether it was another trying day, its only redeeming feature the enticing promise of the courses she would be studying. She had a passion for knowledge.

She did not encounter Edda until near dinner time when she went to her room to freshen up for dinner. To Verna's astonishment, Edda began to talk to her as if there had never been any discord between them. Not that she was warm or friendly, but at least she conversed. "I'm so mad I could scream!" she ranted, as much to herself as to Verna. In fact, Edda didn't look at her at all; unless she had happened to be there to hear it, the rage would have been just so much bitterness wasted on the desert air.

"I wrote ahead and told them I wanted Russian novel and they've gone and put me in a stupid world literature course." She brushed violently at her long sandalwood hair. She still did not actually address Verna; she would have talked to anyone. "And now when I show them their mistake, they try to tell me that 'They're sor-ry'" — she mocked the apology — "that the Russian novel class is full.' Just wait till I tell Uncle Raymond. I would have gone straight to him today but that he's always so busy on registration day." She rattled on and on recounting her own woes.

Verna ventured to put in a remark.

"I would just love to take the world literature course. It sounds so interesting. My English teacher at school — "

"Don't talk to me about interesting literature. All they give here is so puerile. Absolutely juvenile. They still consider Dostoievski modern Russian. The prof is so ancient he's too deaf to have heard that Russia is the coming great power in the world today. Deliver me."

Verna looked puzzled. She was not sure enough of her ground to enter into argument with Edda, but the statement bothered her.

Edda twisted up her hair skillfully, thrust a few pins in and sprayed it thoroughly. Verna had never seen hair spray used. She was not sure whether to be fascinated or disapprove of it. So she said nothing. She polished the dust from her brown oxfords and changed from her brown skirt and white blouse to her brown cotton shirtwaist dress which she had worn on the trip the day before.

Edda cast a glance at her. "You're certainly going

to have to do some shopping for clothes, aren't you!" she stated with a curl of her delicate nostril. Her own clinging sea green jersey sheath was sure not to go unnoticed.

Verna colored and turned away. "We can't afford much," she replied tersely.

Edda gave a little toss of her slim shoulders and her sleek coiffure and went out. The same old smarting, blighting barb fretted in Verna's spirit. She stood in front of the specked mirror a long time. It was true, she decided; she did not have that something attractive about her that most of the other girls here possessed. How could she acquire it? Her father would say, Don't try, it only leads to sin. Her mother would purse her lips and say, Forget it, it isn't worth it. But for the first time Verna faced the hitherto unacknowledged fact that she was not sure at all that it was not worth it. It might turn out to be the anonymous thing she had been longing for, for years. She turned away with a sigh, but a new determination was born of her despair. Something must be done; she didn't know what, but she would find out. She wouldn't cast away her faith that she had been taught, but what was to hinder her having both?

Downstairs, on her forlorn way over to the dining room, she heard her name called. Rose was standing in an open doorway, motioning to Verna to come in.

"We won't keep you," smiled Rose. "I know you're on your way to supper. But I want you to meet Mrs. Ross." The tone of Rose's voice set Mrs. Ross in a special class by herself.

At the very thought of meeting a stranger Verna recoiled inwardly, but Rose slid her arm through Verna's in a sisterly fashion.

Shyly Verna looked up. At first all she noticed was a pair of kind eyes and a smile that gave her the feeling that this charming person knew all there was to know about her and loved her anyway, personally, devotedly. Mrs. Ross was slightly above average height, with softly graying brown hair gracefully coiffured, and a figure that was motherly but not stout.

She laid gentle hands on Verna's shoulders, saying with sincere warmth, "We are so very glad to have you with us, dear. I hope you will feel at home here."

Verna tried to stammer out a response, but the soft-voiced woman chatted on a little, to save the girl having to think up the correct reply. She walked with her to the door. She had a very noticeable limp; one leg was inches shorter than the other. But she started Verna off again to the dining room feeling as if all was well with the world and the college.

When Verna stood with her tray looking for an empty place, the only one she could see vacant was at a large table where four or five girls and fellows were already eating. She placed her tray and drew out her chair. The boy beside her reminded her just a little of her own next older brother. He was husky and big chested, with curly short hair redder than her brother's. They called him Colley.

He greeted her with a careless nod. The others went on talking. Verna hoped she would not be expected to join in the conversation. All she wanted was to be let alone. Where were all her dreams of finding a host of delightful friends in college?

The group was chattering about the day's doings, about the new courses, the profs, and the new students. Verna simply listened.

"I hear the new political science prof is a holy terror," said one. "My cousin had him in Columbia. He's so smart it hurts."

"Yes, and you can't graduate unless you pass his course," moaned a pale-faced girl opposite Verna. "Even if you took political science in another school, you have to take it here."

"New York is your hometown, isn't it, Corbett?" spoke up one of the boys.

The boy next to Verna nodded gloomily. "What if it is? What'll it get me? He never had barbecued chicken in our back yard," he growled. His voice was thick and gruff, like her own brother's. Verna stole another glance at him. Maybe he was as nervous about starting in here as she was. He didn't look studious. She ventured a question.

"Are you a freshman?" She spoke quietly, shy about letting the rest hear. To her it was audacious to begin a conversation. He didn't hear what she said and she had to repeat it. But this time her tongue got tangled up.

"Are you-fresh?" she said, and then blushed and choked. What would he think of her? But he evidently assumed that he had missed the last half of the word, for he replied without interest, "Yes, are you?"

Relieved, she nodded, and that was the end of their sociability.

But the next day when she arrived in the political science class, there he was, sitting to her right in the row ahead of her. He smiled in a comradely fashion and Verna began to realize that she had now two friends — or at least acquaintances — among the boys, and two women friends, Rose and Mrs. Ross.

More students poured in. To her dismay, Edda Wittig was one of them. She took a seat on the front row with confident arrogance. As soon as the instructor arrived she met him at his desk, with a communication that appeared to be confidential. He gave her brief attention. She hovered a minute, then nothing daunted, flounced back to her seat.

Just before the bell rang, in came Sam with a handsome man who was even taller than Sam. He was very straight and carried his gold crowned head with an assured gracious air. He was the sort of person at whose entrance the whole roomful stopped talking and stared. Even the teacher, aware of something new in the atmosphere, looked up from his papers. The newcomer glanced his way and their eyes locked. It was as if there was a challenge, publicly, before them all. The professor, Edward Karpen, unconsciously put up a hand to smooth his tiny mustache, once to the left, once to the right. Then a veil dropped before the younger man's eyes; he inclined his head courteously, the slightest bit, and took his seat.

The whole class sensed that a duel was to be fought at some not too distant date.

Sam had not met the fourth member of their quartet until the afternoon of registration day. Having finished his own affairs, he had promised to help a latecomer try to cut red tape. He was waiting near the desk at the admission office, contemplating his own weekly schedule for the third time, when he heard the names of his roommates read out in a tone unmistakably cultured. Then the voice added, "And Sam Goldman! *That* sounds good!"

Sam glanced up in surprise. The speaker was tall, with hair the color of burnished brass and an almost knightly bearing. His brows were straight, his forehead wide and fearless. His mouth wore a pleasant look, but the jaw gave warning that its owner was not to be lightly pushed around.

Sam decided to reconnoiter. He edged over to the desk as if he were waiting in line himself. With one eye he scanned the form which the tall newcomer was filling out. He was printing his name and address, in the swift, square, legible manuscript letters typical of a clear thinker and a forceful performer.

"William Brewster Lodge
Springfield, Penna. Age 19. Birthplace Boston, Mass. Other colleges attended: New York University 2 yrs."

So here was his fourth roommate!

Ordinarily Sam would have accepted the various items of birth and training as casual facts and let it go at that. But the remarkable tone of voice in which this young man had said "Good!" to Sam's name, intrigued him.

When the newcomer turned away from the counter to take his belated place in the registration line, Sam fell into step beside him.

"This way, Bill. It's shorter." He grinned as the other man looked at him, startled. Sam put out his hand. "Sam Goldman, eavesdropper."

"Well, what do you know! The first guy I meet! How come?" He took Sam's hand in a mammoth grip, piercing him with kindly steady eyes. A slow smile grew on his face and he gave his head a delighted shake. "This is great, old man! We'll have a winter of it."

When Bill and Sam entered the political science class next day both were immediately conscious of the professor's hostility. Not a very auspicious start for getting high grades.

The bell rang, the professor arose and the class quieted down, each one mentally evaluating the person who was to have such great authority over their lives that he could actually hinder them from graduating.

He was slender, fairly tall, and fortyish, with black compelling eyes and a rough pockmarked skin. He had a way of jerking his left shoulder occasionally when he had to pause to find a word. Then, as if to cover the hesitation, he would give a little caress to his finely etched mustache, once to the left, once to the right. He wore a bright red necktie.

The thirty or more students who faced him sat mutely awaiting his disposal of their thoughts and time.

He flashed them a winning smile as he began.

"In this class," he said, "we shall be discussing the various forms of government which have been tried by nations in the past and present, and especially that form of government commonly called democracy which obtains today in the United States of America. We shall want to analyze it from stem to stern, from top

44

to bottom. If there are flaws in it, you are the ones, you of the emerging generation, who will have the privilege and responsibility of correcting them. Your first assignment will be to write a short theme setting forth concisely what you consider is wrong with the world today. Later we shall be more specific and take up the main faults to be found with this country's government. Don't be afraid to express yourself. Think up everything that comes to your mind, and boil it down. We shall take up the themes in class, analyzing and classifying them. We shall consider the best ways to correct the failure of our government as well as of the whole world system. In this class you are going to learn to *think*. Above all see that you keep an open mind and be man enough to change your opinions and prejudices if they turn out to be wrong. Now open your text books and we'll see what others have to say."

At the end of this speech Sam stole a glance at Bill. He was staring straight ahead, expressionless, at the man behind the desk. Sam could not be sure what he was thinking. Sam's newspaper work had taught him to keep his opinions to himself until there was reason to speak. So he kept his own counsel. But he was puzzled. For Sam had a haunting memory of having seen this man before.

CHAPTER 5

"But Rose, she's such a frightful square! She's absolutely quadrilateral. I wouldn't know what to say to her."

Rose smiled at the self-assured little freshman whose blonded forelock was combed into just the proper number of fringes on her untroubled forehead.

"Just remember, Lou, that at one time you were

45

shy and floundering among a lot of strangers. What did you wish people would say to you?"

"Oh, my word! That was so long ago I can't even remember." Sophistication kept its nice balance on her plump shoulders in spite of her shrug. "Well, okay. I'll try. But 'Schiffelgruber!' ugh!" Off she fluttered to attempt her good deed. Rose looked after her with misgivings.

"I picked the wrong one, I guess," she muttered to herself. "She impressed me as rather extrovert, and friendly. But it seems as though every single one of them is all wrapped up in herself." Rose went in search of Mrs. Ross.

"Why?" she demanded of the house mother. "Why are they all so completely selfish?" She spread her hands in a gesture of despair. Mrs. Ross's arms were full of clean linens. An awareness came into Rose's eye and she took them from her. "Question two. Why are you just the opposite? Always running yourself ragged for these kids, doing the menial tasks that really belong to someone else? Where do these go? I'm serious," she insisted. "I want to know why."

The older woman gave her a sober, wistful smile. "*All* we like sheep have gone astray. We have turned everyone to his *own* way, and — " She paused, then put a period to her remark.

Rose flung her a look that was irritated but at the same time unresentful.

"There you go again," she retorted. "You always meet everything I say with the Bible! You know it gets me down, because I can't answer it." She was not angry, only frustrated. "Why do you do it to me?"

"Because you understand," smiled Mrs. Ross enigmatically.

"But I *don't* understand."

"Don't you? If you didn't you wouldn't be so put out about it. The sheets go up to 316. Thank you, dear. You are a great help." The overseer of the

46

ninety girls in Holley Hall East went to her desk and sat down. The conversation was ended.

Slowly and thoughtfully Rose ascended the stairs. What was it about Mrs. Ross that was so delightfully fascinating and — yes, precious? She adored her. The woman never showed any sign of making Rose her pet, never forced her ideas upon her, yet Rose was sure that in any sort of trouble or emergency, she could count on the house mother to be one hundred percent dependable. You didn't meet people like that on every block. This was Rose's third year under her, and she had never yet seen Mrs. Ross make a decision that favored herself. What made her like that? The same old question hovered again at the edge of Rose's consciousness. Could her remarkable charm have anything to do with what Rose had just charged her with — that constant preoccupation with the Bible? She shoved the query aside as she had before, dozens of times. But each time it gained just a little more foothold in the basic foundation of Rose's philosophy.

She finished her errand and took her way with determined steps back to Mrs. Ross's little parlor.

"I've got to ask you one more thing. I know I'm interrupting you terribly."

"That's all right, dear. That's what I'm here for."

"Every time you quote the Bible to me it's from the Old Testament. I recognize it. We had to memorize a lot of that when we were small. Why do you never quote from *your* part? You consider the New Testament the Bible just as much as the Old."

Mrs. Ross smiled again. "Because you have been taught that the Old Testament is the Word of God. And because it doesn't matter which I use. The New is hidden in the Old; the Old explains the New."

Rose frowned in bewilderment. "How could the Old *explain* the New when the New wasn't written yet?"

47

"Only if the same Person authored them both and had the New in mind when he planned the Old. Right?"

Rose flushed; her eyes grew blacker. "There you go. You're trying to prove to me that the New Testament is inspired as much as the Old."

Mrs. Ross looked up from her work with the quiet smile that Rose had learned to love; it had just a bit of a twinkle mixed with the love in it. "You asked me." Then she turned back to her work.

At dinner that evening Sam sought out his sister at the little table where she had sat down a moment with Verna. The girl was alone as usual. Rose had beckoned to another couple of girls going by with their trays. But they had hastily nodded their heads toward another table where there were two empty seats, as if they had promised to sit with the others there. But although they entered into immediate conversation with the others, Rose was quite aware that they had not been expected. She wondered whether Verna noticed.

Behind Sam, and inches taller, was a stranger with a crown of living gold on his head.

"Got someone to look after me, Rosie," grinned Sam. "This is my roommate, Bill Lodge. Bill, my kid sister Rose." He beamed. Sam was proud of his beautiful sister. "Oh, uh — and a classmate of mine, VeeEm," he added.

Verna flashed a grateful glance at Sam and shyly acknowledged the introduction by fluttering her lids. But for Rose the dining room was no more. There were only herself and this stranger who bore himself like one of Arthur's knights and bowed to her as if she had been a princess. She stopped breathing completely to wait for the room to right itself.

Even Sam didn't notice his sister's confusion; he was to busy rediscovering the amber glint in Verna's hair. What a shame the kid was such a square. But she did have some brains; she might turn out not too bad in time. Worth someone's while to work with her. Rose might get somewhere. The kid sure needed some friends to help rub off the corners.

"You aren't eating?" Sam looked at Rose, then at the empty place on the table before her.

Rose shook her head. "I've had mine. I just dropped down here a minute," she murmured, rising. "You want me, Sam?"

"Well, if you're not busy." He nodded to Verna. "You won't mind my taking her away?" He didn't wait for an answer. The three sauntered off together leaving Verna to wonder whether it would ever, ever be her fortune to be picked up like that to saunter off with a congenial group of young people.

Verna had never had a real date. Her father had forbidden dating on the ground that she was too young. Once, two years ago, when she was fifteen, an ugly boy in Sunday school had asked her to go to the picnic with him. But her father had given permission only if they went with the rest of the family, so Verna had chosen to remain at home, reading. If she had not had books, she felt she would have gone mad. She had read everything in the small school library and many classics which her English teacher had lent her. She identified with every heroine; the vicarious thrills provided her only path of escape from monotony. She had always supposed that college would be her box of chocolate coated cherries. But so far, they were not good or even tasteless; they were bitter.

By the time the three young people had reached the sidewalk, Rose was breathing normally. What had come over her? She had never been swept off her feet like this before. This was bound to be a perfectly ordinary young man, of course, just her brother's roommate. Yet she found herself impatient to have another look at his eyes; was it just that they were a deep, deep blue, or had there been an answering gleam in them? She could scarcely wait to look again.

49

"I didn't have half enough to eat," declared Sam. "Let's toddle down to Lasky's and get a hamburger."

All the way down the elm-draped slope to the foot of the campus, Sam conversed about their courses, their profs, and his roommates, but Rose scarcely heard him.

They slid into a booth at the noisy, cluttery little sundry store. Sam took the end of the seat beside his sister, opposite his friend. Rose reached for a menu card, although she knew of old exactly what was on it. She was putting off the exquisite moment when she must look up and face those earnest dark blue eyes again. What would she find there? Surely he was not waiting, too, for her to glance up. She could feel his gaze moving here and there around the room. Then she was aware that it came to rest on her. It was time to look up. She felt as if her lids were lifting great weights, yet she wanted to look at him more than she had ever wanted anything. At last she made it, just a glimmer of a glance. It was all over, like a lightning flash, almost before it began. But it was there. She knew it and he knew it. He dropped his eyes simultaneously with hers. The color rolled up in waves under Rose's creamy skin. She barely managed to stammer out, "Fudge sundae, please," to the waitress.

Rose knew what was happening. She had heard other girls talk; she had watched this happen to others many a time. She had thought it couldn't happen to her. She felt ashamed, as if she had planned it. She despised girls who did that. The normal procedure now would be for this fellow to come upon her in the hall tomorrow and date her; then he would pour out a lot of sentimentality about how he recognized right away that they belonged together, and he would try to take advantage of that one glance as far as she would let him. But he would discover that she knew how to freeze everything in her vicinity for yards around her. She proceeded to do it.

Her chin was inches above its usual position over her pretty neck. Her black eyes glared across the store with loathing at an animated ad of a silky looking fellow operating a new kind of safety razor. She scarcely took part in the boys' conversation.

Sam was quiet on the way back to the dorm. Sam was vaguely aware that something had gone wrong. It must be that Rose didn't approve of his new friend. Queer. She was usually so discerning. Tomorrow he would ask her. Bill must have noticed it; he was rather silent, too. What a pity. He had thought they would hit it off together. You never could tell!

But when Sam finally sought out his sister later in the week, she was uncommunicative.

"Oh, he seemed nice enough," she agreed casually and changed the subject.

The following days were filled with hard work. Sam got a weekend job; Rose was kept fairly busy between her own studies and her work for Mrs. Ross. Verna, rebuffed on every hand, lunged feverishly toward her goal of beating Edda Wittig.

The political science class had proved to be exciting, if not easy. The days their evaluations of the world system were due there were discussions; some waxed hot. It took a good many class periods to cover them all. Most of the students criticized the lack of co-operation among the nations, presenting idealistic cures which Professor Karpen promptly tore to tatters. Some complained of capitalism or imperialism; Sam noted that Karpen warmed up to these. Many papers were trite, unimaginative; the writers had that made known to them in no uncertain terms, whereupon they grovelled in mortification since the majority of the class were freshmen and scared anyway.

Sam had ventured to bring up the subject one evening when the four fellows were lying in bed talking.

"Where do you think this guy Karpen stands?" He had fallen into the habit, perhaps unconsciously, of addressing most of his conversation to Bill Lodge, since Corbett never bothered to have opinions, and Snead, he decided, merely climbed on to the nearest band-wagon.

As Bill did not answer immediately, Corbett spoke up in his dull bass. "He'll be okay with me if he passes me."

"Heh heh," chortled Snead. "Me too. I'm dumb. Heh heh."

"What do you make of him, Bill?" persisted Sam.

"I'll know better after class tomorrow. He's up to L's. I'll be surprised if he likes my paper. He seemed to appreciate yours, though. He didn't jump down your throat like he has some of them. You had some terrific points, Sam."

"D'ja think so? Thanks. I wanted to say a lot more. Maybe sometime I will. I'm not sure it's worth it, though. Funny thing, I keep thinking I've seen the guy before somewhere."

No one answered, and soon there were snores. Sam wondered what Bill would have to say in his report. He had discovered that Bill was unusually keen, a thinker, with plenty of facts to back up his statements. He was glad to have a guy like Bill to pal around with. Bill seemed to like him, too. Sam had not yet discovered why Bill had said "Good" to Sam's name that first day. Sometime he'd ask him, maybe. Funny how Rose hadn't taken to him. You never could tell about girls.

The next morning Karpen began the class by calling on Lodge. His tone seemed sharp, even apprehensive. His small white hand tapped nervously on his desk with a red pencil.

Bill walked to the front as the others had done. His step was firm and unhurried. There was nothing of the fidgety apprehension that marked some who had stood up there reading their thoughts out nakedly before the rest.

52

"There are four things wrong with the world system." Bill spoke with quiet authority. "First, the Jewish people are out of place." A quick gasp could be heard here and there around the room. Ears pricked up. Something tightened about Sam's heart.

"Many of them are still scattered throughout the world; they should be settled at home in Israel in the land that is rightfully theirs." Sam drew a long breath and relaxed.

"Second, the devil is out of place. He is walking to and fro in the world; he should be chained in the bottomless pit."

Snickers here and there.

"Third, the Church of Jesus Christ is out of place. She is still under persecution here on the earth; she belongs with the Lord. And fourth, the Lord Jesus Christ is still in heaven; He should be here on earth ruling the world through the Jewish nation at Jerusalem."

Without further comment Bill took his seat.

There was dead silence a long moment. Then suddenly raucous laughter burst out, growing louder and wilder. Mr. Karpen was throwing himself back in his swivel chair, beside himself with derision.

Several of the class, including Edda and Corbett, joined him, roaring their ridicule one above another to be heard and accounted intelligent by him. Only a few waited in mute disgust until the uproar should cease.

Sam was one of these. He was angry for Bill's sake. Bill didn't have to take this. But Bill sat through it all, apparently unconcerned.

At last it seemed there was nothing more to laugh at and the mockery subsided as suddenly as it had started. Mr. Karpen glared at Bill. It was obvious that he was trying to devise the perfect squelch. Varied shades of amusements and scorn flitted across his coarsely handsome face. Finally he said,

"Students, this is going to be a most interesting year. We have a real live zealot in our midst. One doesn't often meet the species any more. It may be that before the winter is over we will all be sitting atop the Tower in our bed sheets waiting for the end of the world." He clasped his hands piously. Another roar of laughter.

Bill showed no sign of anger or of shame. He merely drew a deep breath and sat there without fidgeting, looking straight at Mr. Karpen. This apparently roused the man to a frenzy. He sprang up and began to shake his finger at the students, shouting,

"Repent, ye sinners, and be converted. Know ye not that the wages of sin is death, and hell — and all that sort of rot?" He exploded with glee again over his own parody. "Somebody bring some sawdust. Let's go down the sawdust trail. Come to Jesus, friends. Come now. Tomorrow may be too late. Who is on the Lord's side?"

Suddenly, impulsively, Verna stood to her feet. "I am," she said trembling in the sudden hush.

Colley Corbett turned full around and stared at her. Then he snorted. All at once Verna remembered that her hair was not combed stylishly, and she was a country Dutch "square." Edda twisted in her seat and smothered a shriek, holding her head in her hands. "Oh, my word. Don't blame me, folks."

Several others called out wisecracks. Through it all Bill still sat with his arms folded. Verna had taken her seat again, choking down excited sobs, staring straight ahead of her and blinking fast, her face as red as fire.

In the midst of the hubbub, while Karpen was still flinging his arms and calling on sinners to come forward, Sam got to his feet.

He stood until Karpen, with an ill-concealed sneer, motioned for quiet.

"Sir," said Sam in a clear voice, "I signed up for a political science class. This seems to me more like a zoo. We all understood that the assignment was to

54

write what we thought. Whether we all agree with Bill's ideas or not, it is evident that he has carried out the assignment in good faith. I think that not only Bill deserves an apology, but God."

Sam sat down. The room suddenly teemed with embarrassed awe.

Karpen, chagrined, shrugged his shoulders and caressed his mustache, once to the left, once to the right. He put one shoulder up and burlesqued, "'*De gustibus non disputandum est,*' as the old lady said when she kissed the cow. Class, we have been reproved, Let's *try* to control ourselves." But the sneer had not faded from his full red lips when through the silence of the embarrassing moment came Edda Wittig's harsh, throaty tones: "I always did *love* kikes!"

The professor suppressed a smirk and hastily flipped the pages of his book as if to change the subject and get on with the class, but Sam arose commandingly and took a step that placed him directly in front of Edda.

With a courteous bow he said clearly, "May I remind this young person of the words of the great Disraeli: 'When your ancestors were savages in an unknown land, mine were priests in the temple of Solomon.'"

He sat down. Bill wore a broad grin. Suddenly the rest of the class broke into hilarious laughter. Edda's usually pale cheeks flamed; she was so angry that she trembled all over. Mr. Karpen put on a conciliatory expression, ran his fingers down the roll book and spoke over the din. "All right, let's get back to work. L, L, M. Mr. Martin, what have you to give us today?"

The class settled down once more to humdrum. There was a sour taste in their mouths. Sides had to be taken. The noisy majority longed for gossip. The quiet minority would have much to live down.

On the way out, in the corridor, Sam muttered to Bill, "*Now* I remember where I saw that guy before!"

CHAPTER 6

"Why did you do it, Bill?"

The top was down on Bill's convertible and the sun was nearly at its zenith, blazing away at his gold hair as if doing its best to turn it to flame. Sitting half a head lower in the car, Sam noted the three straight lines of Bill's profile, his brow and nose and chin. No compromise in any one of them. Whatever course Bill Lodge decided on, that he would stick to, it was plain. Sam was vaguely aware that he desperately wanted Bill to ring true. His liking for him had increased since that day at the registration desk. Sam was puzzled.

After the uproarious political science class, the two fellows had with one accord gravitated to Bill's car and headed for the hills a few miles away.

Bill did not answer immediately. He parked in the shade of a huge maple where they could look far over the valley. The sky was a peaceful blue, decorated with soft white pillows of clouds, in no hurry to go anywhere.

Without looking at his friend, Bill finally replied, "Why shouldn't I?"

Sam frowned. "Because you're not like that. You wouldn't deliberately start a riot without a reason for it."

"I didn't."

"What was your reason, then? You wanted to see Karpen make an ape of himself?"

"No."

Sam frowned again and waited for Bill to explain. When he did not, Sam repeated, "Well, why did you do it? You surely didn't *believe* all that."

56

"Why not?"

"Well, because it's crazy. Fantastic. Fanatical. It belongs to people who try to be different just to attract attention. You're not like that. I don't get you. If you don't want to explain, okay." Sam allowed a little edge to creep into his tone.

Bill turned and smiled down at him. For such a giant, it was a gentle, understanding smile. "Don't get your fur up, son. I'm not trying to be mysterious. I just meant what I said. I do believe it. I wouldn't have flung it at them like that if it hadn't been an assignment, but the guy asked for it. I wasn't going to make up a lot of rubbish. It's a lot easier to tell the truth. He may give me an F for it but that's beside the point."

Sam stared at his friend. Bill made no further comment, just gazed off at the white clouds, and the look on his face was one of deep content, which puzzled Sam to exasperation.

"Well," exclaimed Sam at last, "at least I admire your nerve. I guess you do believe it."

Bill grinned again. It was as if he were waiting for Sam to push a certain button that would release his thoughts, but he was not rushing him. He said nothing. They sat long minutes, each doing his own thinking.

Then Sam spoke, as if he had made a decision.

"Did you know I was Jewish, Bill?"

Bill nodded. "Yes. I knew it before I met you. In fact, I asked for a Jewish roommate."

Sam looked stunned. "Is that why you said 'Good' when you read my name that first day?"

"Yep," agreed Bill evenly.

Why?"

This time Bill didn't grin. He turned to Sam with utmost seriousness. "It's a long story. But you asked for it; you might as well have it. I had a wonderful father," he began, his face softening. "He was strong, and homely, and honest. He taught me obedience and

57

loyalty. He died when I was ten. After that, my mother, a glorious redhead, who loved him intensely — Mother has always been intense to the point of being uncontrollable — " Bill's voice dropped low as if he disliked speaking so of his mother. Then he went on gently. "She got — well, she's in an institution now. But for several years there was no one to tell me where to get off. We always had plenty of money, and I had a blast." He sighed deeply.

"I'd give a lot to have those years blotted out. In fact — " Bill broke off and flashed Sam a radiant smile — "they *are* blotted out; but I never could have done it myself. I even had a brush with the law; it just missed being serious. The trouble was, I have my mother's way of going headlong into whatever I do. I was wild as a March hare. I didn't wise up until a couple of years ago, one morning, when I woke up and saw bars around me. I found that there had been a murder the night before. Another fellow who was with us was tried and sentenced to life. He was only nineteen. I knew it could just as well have been me. We were all drunk."

Sam saw Bill's throat muscles working and he swallowed hard. Sam could scarcely picture this handsome, clean-cut giant in such a situation.

"After that I tried to go straight, but it was too easy not to. This other fellow's trial dragged on a long time and I got so I dreaded to read about it in the papers, I felt so guilty about it myself. But there was nothing I could do for him.

"I was getting more desperate all the time, trying to find out what I could live for, and why I was outside of jail. I wasn't any better than he was." Bill hesitated. "I don't know how to tell you what happened next. No, it wasn't any bright light and I didn't hear voices," he grinned as he saw Sam's apprehensive eye on him. "I was eating a hamburger at a little downtown joint in New York. A fellow came in and sat down at my table. He ordered a burger too, I remember. He looked — something like you, only shorter. He had dark hair and black eyes. He was Jewish. He had a pile of books that he set on the table. I saw there were math and physics. I'd always liked those in high school, so we got talking. He was a student at N.Y.U. He asked a lot of questions about what I was doing, and why I wasn't in college. I hedged, but I think he guessed a lot between the lines. He was a real guy, nice and friendly, and boy, was he smart! We got to talking relativity and space and that sort of thing. It made me eager to learn some more. Well, he invited me to go with him to a bull session that night where he said there were a bunch of fellows, N.Y.U. students, who liked to get together to talk about all sorts of things. I didn't have anything else to do, so I went. Whew! What a deal! If I had known what it was I never would have gone near it. But," he paused again and looked off to the clouds, "I'll never get done being thankful I went."

Bill was so serious and remained silent so long that Sam egged him on. "Well, *give,* man. What happened?"

"Hunh! You'll never believe it. It was a prayer meeting!"

Bill took pleasure in Sam's horrified expression.

"Yep, a prayer meeting. And the fellows all got together and discussed the Bible. None of them knew too much about it — I've learned enough to understand that now — but they were digging in. I found that I had to unlearn a lot of fool ideas I'd picked up in school and here and there about what the Bible *really* says. Anyway, it was interesting. I even promised to go again. Not only that, but I decided to enroll in the university, come second semester. I had finished high school, so it was no problem.

"Well, I went to those meetings regularly, and I found I was wanting more and more to know what it was that these guys had. I had never come on any-one like them before. Why, they'd go out of their way to help you, me, or anybody, any time of the day or night. And they weren't all in a dither about the world and tomorrow, and Russia, and whether their families ought to build underground shelters and that sort of tripe. They had real peace of mind. I mean it. Well, it got so I was worse worried over being what I was than I had ever been before, so one night, all by myself, I just got down on my knees and poured it all out to God. I asked Jesus Christ to do for me what it says in the Bible He will do. I had never realized before what a sinner I was — not only the carousing around, but paying no attention to God — that was worst of all, trying to run my own life with-out Him. So I asked Him to cleanse me of sin. And He did. And I found out what peace is, for the first time. After that, the Bible began to make sense. That's where I learned what I gave this morning." Bill turned squarely to Sam for the first time. "So now you have it. Let's go back."

"Wait a minute, Bill." Sam was still uneasy. "You haven't told me yet why you wanted me for a room-mate."

"Maybe you won't understand, Sam, but I have — well, at least three reasons. It was a Jew who put me in the way of finding peace with God. It was a Jew, Jesus Christ, who made peace with God for me. And it was Jews who wrote the Book that tells the whole story. I just love your people, that's all."

Sam stared at him a long time.

"Bill," he said, wonderingly, "I believe you are the first Gentile who ever said that to me. And you mean it! You may have some crazy ideas. I'll look into that later. But I'm with you." He put out his hand and Bill took it in his immense grip.

Bill started the car and turned homeward.

"I'd like to twist that guy Karpen's silly red tie until he chokes!" said Sam after a mile or two.

"Oh, better let him hang himself with it," grinned Bill. "He will, in time. By the way, you said something about having known him before, didn't you?"

"I've had a hunch all along and this morning it hit me. I worked on a newspaper for a year or two. Started as printer's helper and then they let me do a little cub reporting. Once they sent me to cover a school quarrel between some members of the P.T.A. and the school superintendent. It seems the parents had complained that the kids weren't being taught right. They accused the superintendent of trying to change the whole framework. The school board fired him and he played martyr. His name was Karpinsky. He had been named in another state as one of several teachers who had refused to sign a loyalty oath. I'd swear it was this same guy. He didn't wear a mustache then, and he was a good deal heavier. But his face has haunted me ever since the class started."

"Could be," agreed Bill. "He'll bear watching. Did you notice how he emphasized finding fault with the U.S. government? Not that it hasn't got its faults, but to deliberately set a lot of kids to criticizing the country is not my idea of constructive teaching."

"That's why I asked you that night what you thought of him," reminded Sam. "You wouldn't stick your neck out."

Bill grinned. "How did I know you weren't pink yourself?"

They had reached the campus. Students were streaming over to the dining room.

"You'll be in for some plain and fancy bullyragging, Bill," warned Sam anxiously.

"Okay. So be it," he shrugged unconcernedly. "But say, who was the stouthearted gal with the poor judgment to speak out of turn this morning? Wasn't that

61

the amber-haired beauty I met in the dining room one night with your sister?"

Sam chuckled. Bill was such an odd combination of propriety and dry humor.

"Yes! You ought to talk to her some time. She's a character. Square, but she's really got what it takes." There was a measure of grudging admiration in his tone.

Just at that moment the amber-haired beauty was in the library finishing a letter home. She had not written before, except a postcard to report that she had arrived. Her father had warned her, "Don't you be spendin' your money on stamps yet. No news'll be good news. Once a week is enough." Her mother had looked distressed, and Verna's rebellious impulse was to write every day, but she knew better than to overstep a law her father laid down. That would only make trouble for her mother.

It was not an easy letter to write. She longed to pour out on paper all the loneliness and bitter disappointment of the past days. But of course that was out of the question. Pride, if nothing else, forbade it. So she used one page in describing the beautiful grounds and buildings. Then she told them how nice Rose had been to her and how charming she was. She described Mrs. Ross. "You needn't worry, mother," she added. "She is the sort you would like. She looks after all of us."

She avoided carefully the fact that she had met and chatted with a perfectly strange young man on the train; and there was no mention of her roommate. Wait until she could say something fit to write about her, if that time ever came. She closed by telling of the fine young man who had given the Bible prophecy report in class. "Many of them didn't like it. They laughed at him, but when the teacher asked who was on the Lord's side, I stood up." Verna's conscience bothered her just a little after she wrote that last. She was perfectly aware that it gave just the opposite impression from the true facts, but she knew also that it would encourage her parents. After all, not a word of it was untrue.

Just to send a cheery word to her little brother, she added, "Tell Ricky that big people sometimes spill things, too. A girl upset her whole tray full of dinner on the dining room floor the first night."

Suddenly it came over her that she was actually seeing that horrible disaster as a joke. Would all of this wilderness turmoil seem funny some day? With a somewhat lighter heart she mailed her letter and went to lunch.

It did not take long for the grapevine to carry the day's news. Bill had already become a familiar figure around the campus because of his unusual looks and his outstanding bearing. By lunch time he was a marked man. Considerable joshing went on at various tables. Sides had been taken but the issue in fact was whether a student's admiration for Bill himself was sufficient to outweigh dislike of notoriety.

Bill ate his hearty lunch nonchalantly, merely grinning when someone tossed a jibe at him. Sam marvelled; Bill was so difficult to classify. He was anything but square, but — there was that peculiar angle of his. On the whole, however, Bill's stock went up several points.

Eventually the rumors reached Rose. At the mention of Bill's name she was alert. Rose had struggled heroically to forget the electric instant when she met him. It was so humiliating to think that she was no more mature and self-possessed than the greenest freshman. Yet she found herself craving a glimpse of him, always scanning the hurrying figures on campus for a bright gold gleam above the other drab heads. She wondered if he had forgotten the charged moment. Had it been for him just another conquest among many?

Her first impulse, when she learned of the uproar, was to call her brother, for she knew that they were classmates under Mr. Karpen. But she did not trust herself to ask Sam about his friend. Sam knew her too well. He would be able to read between the lines too cannily. So she went to Mrs. Ross.

"I hear that there was quite a hubbub in one of Mr. Karpen's classes today," she ventured while she and Mrs. Ross were sorting supplies.

"Oh?" was the response. That was the only trouble with Mrs. Ross. *She never will go out on a limb with her opinions; she always makes me commit myself first,* thought Rose. *She's very wise to be that way, and I admire her for it. But she's going to make me be the one to state the case, and I don't want to. As sure as I do I'll find myself on the spot.*

Rose tallied a list with the towels she had counted. Then she tried again. "Yes, I hear that a new student came out with some outlandish ideas he claims come from the Bible and Karpen laughed him to scorn. They had quite a riot. And our little country Dutch girl stood up and took sides with him. For all her inferiority complex she must have courage."

"That sounds very interesting," returned Mrs. Ross.

Rose made a sound of exasperation. "For such a precious person you can be the most aggravating!" declared Rose good-humoredly. "I'm perfectly positive that you know all about this bit and you're just trying to lead me on!"

Mrs. Ross chuckled. "And I'm succeeding?"

"I suppose you are, hang it all! You want to force me to tell what was said and then you will quote the Bible to prove that the whole thing is true."

"Not unless it is true. You wouldn't want me to do that. And if it is true, wouldn't you want to know it?"

"There you go. I can't get out of an argument like that. All right, here it is, as I heard it." Rose had taken pains to get the story from several sources and she was able to give rather accurately the gist of Bill's talk.

Mrs. Ross made no response.

"Well?" persisted Rose. "Aren't you going to say anything?"

"What do you want me to say?"

"Oh, what *makes* you like that? You know perfectly well that I want to know whether you think that's what the Bible says."

"And if I say yes, what will you do?"

Rose thought a moment. Then she answered very seriously, "I suppose I would either have to give up thinking so much of *you,* or ask you to show me in the Bible where you get it all."

"And that is quite a dilemma?" Mrs. Ross could be so tantalizing!

"Actually, yes," replied Rose. "You evidently don't realize how very much I think of you, or else you don't realize how very much it would necessarily mean to me if I was convinced that those things are really true." Rose's tone showed how deeply she had considered the problem. "I just don't know," she went on, "what it would do to my family if — " her words trailed off.

Mrs. Ross stopped her work and limped over to the girl. "I do realize, dear," she said gently. "What you think of me, Rose, is beside the point. But I will say this, that I can show you in the Bible, yes, even in the Old Testament, that these things are true. It is you who will have to make your decision as to whether you want to see them or not." She left a light kiss on the top of Rose's hair and took her hitch-hobbling way out of the room.

Rose was in a turmoil. She sat for a long time in Mrs. Ross's little parlor, looking out the window. The sun was low; it sent a narrow shaft piercing straight through the elms into the little room. Rose watched the particles of dust in the air dance in the light. Was that the way each individual person looked to God? Weren't human beings, made of the dust, mere specks floating in the essence of eternity? Why was that one speck next to its neighbor? What law brought it into that juxtaposition? Was there a law that governed those specks? Or did they just happen to be where they were? What did the word "happen" mean, anyway? Each one of those particles must have taken its place as the result of some outside influence, a breeze, or heat, or some unknown power. Why had she, for instance, Rose Goldman, been thrust into this school, and under the influence of a charmer like Mrs. Ross? Why had she met that divinely attractive young man last week? What influence had brought them together? Would they ever meet again? Einstein had proposed electricity as the power that holds the universe together. Was the thrill of the meeting with Bill Lodge an expression of that power? Or could it possibly be that a thinking, loving Being had planned it? That would be in line with what Mrs. Ross believed. Desperate with her thoughts, at last she strolled outdoors.

It was time for the evening meal but she had no appetite. The problem that she had forced Mrs. Ross to put into words must be faced. But she found herself not ready to face it. She must escape — where? She started to walk. Most of the students were indoors, at dinner. She took her way swiftly up to the broad flat rock at the very top of the hill behind the dorm — Romance Rock, it had been lovingly dubbed by former generations of students. At the foot of a great elm, overlooking the valley, there was a stone bench. Rose dropped down on it and gazed off at the sunset. Nearly an hour she sat there, sometimes weeping, sometimes trying to pray. Thinking, thinking, thinking.

The sun had all but disappeared; dusk was ready to creep up even to that high point. Then she heard footsteps. Some couple, probably, coming for a few

moments before they must part, with "sweet sorrow."
Rose jumped up and sprang down the rough steps cut
jaggedly into the rock.

But she was too late. The intruder had reached the
top. The last ray of the sun reached a finger through
the elm and laid it on the burnished waves of his
hair.

Rose caught her breath. "Bill!"

In an instant the light blazed up in his eyes. They
stood in amazement, staring at each other. Then Rose
broke the moment with a ripple of a laugh. "You
like this place, too?" She tried desperately to set the
atmosphere back on the casual basis, but it would not
stay there.

He nodded. "It's wonderful — *now!*" he added,
never taking his eyes from her.

Rose's breath took a power dive and righted itself
again. She snatched at a remark — any remark. "How
did you know I was here?" How silly. He obviously
didn't.

"You had to be!" he smiled. "This was the end of
the trail. I was afraid there would be no end till —
tomorrow."

"Tomorrow?" she questioned. "What's tomorrow?"

"It's always what comes after today, isn't it?" He
smiled again, enigmatically. She started to ask for an
explanation, but he broke in. "Look here, you haven't
had dinner, have you?"

"How did you know?"

"I guessed."

"Why, no-o. I wasn't hungry."

"Neither was I. But now I'm ravenous. Let's go
somewhere and eat. Are you free for awhile?"

"Until eight-thirty," she lilted.

He took her hand and led her down the steep way.
Neither felt any need of words.

All the way to his car they walked silently, just delighting in being together. He helped her in and they
drove away.

CHAPTER 7

That afternoon Edda Wittig stood tall, slim and stylish, in the dean's office, an assured smirk on her red lips as she waited for her uncle to answer her. She knew that she had a gift for putting people on the spot and she enjoyed using it.

The man behind the big desk was nervously fingering a pencil, turning it end for end, end for end, examining the point, and then the eraser. Raymond Wittig was tall and slender, like Edda. His face was thin and his nose, rather precipitous, was inclined to slant obliquely; yet he was not an unhandsome man. His hair, platinum like Edda's, waved back from a fine intelligent forehead.

Just now he was frowning a little and working his lips.

"I don't see how I could make an exception in your case, Edda," he concluded. "I've already turned down several others. This whole problem of roommates is really out of my area."

"You know very well that you can step in when you choose to," she prodded.

He gave a wan uncertain smile that was meant to be conciliatory. "After all, I've always considered you a fairly capable young lady, quite competent to handle difficult situations. You are a psychology major; maybe you can put into practice some of your new found wisdom on this poor inexperienced child to good effect. Why not use her as a project, a case study?" He sat up, pleased with himself for having come up on the spur of the moment with such a neat and practical solution to Edda's complaint about her roommate. It was his job to find solutions, and he usually had no difficulty with other students, but his own niece was continually presenting problems that were somehow more vexing than most.

Edda was never one to be outdone. "Oh, of course I had considered that already," she boasted with a supercilious toss of her sleek head. "Actually it doesn't appeal to me, but I suppose if you refuse to co-operate I'll just have to make the best of it. I have no doubt I could do something with her, especially if I could get some psych credit for it. Very well," she flirted her thin shoulders in disdain, "I'll probably try it, but don't blame me for what may happen!" She gave a hard laugh and went out. Actually the idea was brand new to her, and it appealed to her exaggerated opinion of her own powers. She narrowed her gray-green eyes as she departed.

Dean Wittig sat for some time knitting his brows. He had hoped that George would not choose to send his daughter to the school where he had begun to make a fair name for himself. Edda had always been a difficult child, not particularly likable, even when she was small. Psychologists had told her parents that there must be some frustration that made their daughter so consistently unhappy and sometimes even sadistic. They had offered to use hypnotism to uncover a possible deep-seated injury to her subconscious. But Edda's father had pooh-poohed their pedantic advice. "Mere chauvinism! Nothing in the world the matter except that her mother's spoiled her rotten," he stated bluntly. The professional counsel accordingly shifted emphasis and went to work on the parents' relationship. It was shortly after that that Edda's mother departed. Her father sighed and did his worrying over Edda by himself. His brother Raymond pitied him but how could he sympathize when he had no children of his own, not even a wife?

George tried hard to make up to the unloved little girl for the loss of a mother. A fairly successful banker, he gave her everything except discipline and a good example. Those two items cost more than he was prepared to pay. After she had fretted her way through high school, he decided that he was a failure; his brother, having been trained to guide the young, ought to be able to undo some of the damage.

So Edda had matriculated at the state college where she would supposedly be under the all wise eye of her paternal uncle. She had spent her first year making A's and enemies; it seemed as if she was off to a fine start on the same track for the second year. Raymond had long been aware that his niece carried on many an ignoble operation illicitly. That had been her way since she was small. If he could only learn to manage her, she could be useful to him. But he would certainly have to keep close watch on her. He made a note on his personal pad, which he kept in his pocket, not on his desk.

As Edda made her way back to the library to study, her steps became more and more confident. She took a comfortable seat in the outer lounge with a book in front of her eyes. But her mind was not on it. She was letting her thoughts run riot over the various methods that presented themselves for dealing effectively with those persons about her whom she wished to use or to humiliate. There were certain ones who had been thorns in her flesh from the very first. At the top of the list was Sam Goldman. When she had them well classified she selected certain plans from among the rest and set them down on mental three by five cards, as it were, to do her particular type of human research. Personality study, she would call it, and who knew but she might be able actually to weave the whole scheme into a most rewarding paper that would bring a gleam to the eye of the psychology professor, besides giving her many hours and even weeks of her own special kind of pleasurue.

By the time Edda was ready to go back to her room

to freshen up for dinner she was in high spirits. She found Verna seated at her little maple desk, struggling with calculus, her whole attitude drooping with discouragement and loneliness.

Edda smiled.

"You look bushed," she said in a friendly tone.

It was such a change from the cold ostracism Verna had learned to expect that she looked up at her roommate, startled. Edda was actually smiling.

The older girl glanced down at the page of figures. With superior sophomore skill she flicked a pencil a moment down through a column of figures.

"Here's your trouble." She pinpointed the knot in the complex tangle. "Go back to the rule at the beginning of the chapter." She made the problem look easy. Verna stared at her with awe.

"You are really good at math, aren't you!"

The bit of admiration was just what was needed to consummate Edda's feeling of intoxication. Even her despised roommate was almost bearable when she praised her. And the improved relationship paved the way for her new psychological project.

"Oh, it never was hard for me." She gave her own peculiar superior toss to her head. "But I'm sure you will be able to get it, too. You are willing to work. Most girls aren't."

The unwonted praise from Edda fairly overwhelmed the lonely little country Dutch girl.

"But you look terribly tired. I'll bet you've boned here all afternoon, haven't you?"

Verna nodded. "I didn't realize it was getting so late. I really oughtn't to take time for dinner tonight. I still have an English theme to write."

"Oh, don't take it so hard," advised Edda. "Come on, get yourself fixed up and eat a good dinner. It will rest you and you'll be able to work much better. Yes, go ahead," she urged, for Verna simply stared in amazement at her. "Wash your face in good cold water

71

and come back here. I'm going to do your hair a new way."

Dazed and completely bewildered, the girl obeyed.

"Sit down here in front of the mirror," commanded Edda when she returned. "You have gorgeous hair, did you know it?" Skillfully she brushed the long amber waves while she chatted on, fully aware of the dazzling net of astonishment she was deliberately weaving about her unsuspecting companion.

"Let's do something new and startling." She ran a swift part down the back of Verna's head and swept one whole side of her hair into a neat coy bun over her ear. She did likewise with the other side, then stood off and evaluated her handiwork.

"That's stunning!" she exclaimed in her low throaty, impressive voice. "They won't know you when you walk into the dining room. What fun! Come on."

But the daughter of Mr. and Mrs. Schiffelgruber suddenly sounded an inner alarm. Surprised and pleased as Verna was to have her former enemy suddenly show such interest in her, old habits of conservative thought reared up and inhibited her. She could see her grandmother's stern, shocked look.

"Oh, I couldn't!" she cried in dismay. "Not like this!" She put up her hands as if in shame before her face. Then realizing that she must sound quite unappreciative, she became confused and tried to apologize. "Oh, I didn't mean it's not nice," she cried. "I mean, it's awfully kind of you to take the trouble. And you're so clever with it. But oh, I'd feel terrible going out among people like this. It looks so—oh, I just don't know how to say it."

Edda shrugged. "Okay. Have it your own way," she returned coldly. "Be as square as you choose. See if I care." She marched out of the room.

Verna was panic-stricken. What had she done? This girl had at last become friendly and she had rebuffed her. Had she antagonized her, hurt her beyond repair?

72

She wanted to rush out and ask her forgiveness, but even if she did, she could not picture Edda as being kind and forgiving. Not yet, in spite of her about-face tonight. That was probably just a passing whim. She would be colder than ever after this. Oh, why hadn't she been able to meet the situation in a normal, sensible way, as other girls would? Did any other girl ever make such a mess of her life as she was doing? Then the thought came, were other girls trying to live the Christian life that she had been brought up to feel was the only life worth living? Actually, however, was it wrong to change the way she wore her hair? Why would God care? Suppose she had always worn it that way? Then it wouldn't have seemed so dramatic, such an unwarranted departure from what she had been brought up to. All the traditions of parents and grand-parents had risen up to scream caution to her when she first saw herself in the mirror. But she had to admit, as she gazed at her own image, that it was a very becoming and attractive way to wear hair. "After all, God gave me my hair," she told the girl in the looking glass, "and He never said, 'This is the way you are to comb it.'"

After long minutes of wrestling with herself, she thought of having hurt the feelings of a girl who had tried to be kind and help her won out. Slowly, with a ghastly feeling of uncertainty, she opened the door and went downstairs and over to the dining room.

Most of the students had finished when she arrived. She did not see Edda, nor anyone she knew. After the first few minutes of stiffness, when she imagined that everyone was staring at her, she managed to take a deep breath and discover that no one was paying the slightest attention to her or her hairdo. She ate her dinner in a daze and went back to her room to study.

Edda was not there.

Edda did not come in until long after the lights were supposed to be out. How she managed to get into the

73

building so late was a mystery. Verna wondered whether it was because she was the dean's niece; perhaps they had given her a house key and special privileges.

When she did return she switched on the light. She never made any attempt to consider whether anyone else wanted a light on. Verna stirred. Sleepily she opened one eye and said,

"Edda, I'm sorry I acted so silly. I did go over to dinner. I think my hair looks nice that way. Please forgive me."

"Skip it!" responded Edda crudely. But she gave a triumphant little smile to herself while her back was turned. It worked. There would be more encounters to write up for her project later on, too.

"Where you been?" inquired Verna trying to force herself to crawl out of her shell.

"None of your business," returned Edda. "On a date. What do you think?"

"Oh." At the rebuff Verna's voice faded away in disappointment. She turned over and apparently went to sleep. But she was struggling with tears. How was one to understand the moods of such an inconstant creature?

It was common talk by the end of the next day that Edward Karpen, political science professor, had dated Edda Wittig.

The quiet convertible sped through the dusk on soft shod feet. Neither of the two in the front seat spoke for several miles. Bill was struggling to keep his equilibrium. Never in all the wildest of his escapades had he ever met a girl like this one. He wanted to ride on and on into the fading sunset with her by his side. She seemed so one with him that he felt no need for words.

But Rose was struggling to find words. She felt as if she simply must blanket, by a conventional remark, the fire that had sprung up in them both; even the weather

74

would do. She gazed out at the hills, and across the valley where a veil of mist was creeping gently up to draw a curtain across the thousand lives that were living themselves out under the roofs of the placid village. Nothing but banality occurred to her to say about it. This that had happened to the two of them was so much more than trite. She let her glance wander over the valley to the sky.

"Look!" she breathed, conventional conversation forgotten. There, hung just above the highest hill, was a silver cradle of a moon, and hovering over it as if poised to lean down for a kiss, was the evening star.

Bill glanced where she pointed and slowed the car almost to a stop. He looked from the scene to her, and back, then down at her again. Then he smiled.

"I'm glad you like my moon," he said softly, and drove on.

Rose found her heart in her throat again and no ordinary words would come to her mind.

Before long they turned into a half circle drive where soft lights gleamed behind wide spreading oaks. The building was low and rambling, with cozy rustic seats among plantings here and there on the unroofed entrance porch.

A pleasant hum of quiet voices and the clink of glass and silver sounded a cordial invitation to dine.

Suddenly Rose put her hands up to her hair in the characteristic feminine gesture. "Oh, I'm not dressed to go into a place like this," she demurred. "I thought we'd go down to Lasky's or the drug store."

"You don't belong in Lasky's, or the drug store," smiled Bill. "You do belong here. And you look lovely. You couldn't look anything but lovely wherever you were."

Rose blushed and dropped her eyes again from the worship she saw in his.

"But I don't even have a comb," she protested. "I ought to freshen up a little."

"If you must, here—would you be willing to use mine?" Hesitatingly he took it from his pocket. "I'll wait here."

Rose was gone only a few minutes and when she came back he complimented her once more with his eyes as he led her to a secluded table where a rose colored light could play on her face.

She was dressed in pale clinging ashy pink. It seemed to him that she stood out as the one lovely flower in a roomful of weeds.

"Lobster Newburg?" he questioned her as the waiter stood poised to take their order.

Rose nodded. "I've never had it," she confided with a sheepish little smile after the man had gone. "But I'm sure it'll be good."

Rose looked about her. There were not many in the dining room. The tables were set far apart to ensure a sense of privacy. The few diners seemed to be quiet spoken, unostentatiously dressed. Rose drew a deep, wistful breath. She had always longed to enjoy some of these finer things of gracious living. It was typical of one of the Goldman family that she wished the others could have a taste of it, too. She turned back to her companion. His eyes were still upon her, and his look made the pink steal up again in her cheeks.

"It's lovely here." She tried again to make commonplace remarks do what they should. But they fell so flat.

"Have you ever read the book of Esther in the Bible?" Bill was very serious. His eyes never left her.

"Why, I believe I did, once long ago. Why?"

"You remind me so much of her," he said solemnly. "Surely you have spent 'six months with oil of myrrh and six months with sweet odors,' haven't you?"

Rather mystified, she leaned forward on the table, her smooth olive hands clasped beneath her chin as she stared at him, smiling a little. She wore her long black

76

hair in two braids, caught up around her shapely head like a coronet.

"My mother's name is Esther," she said. "I always liked the name."

"Is it really?" he cried in delight. "Then you ought to have an Uncle Mordecai."

Her laugh was fascinating; soft and low, bubbling up gently. "As a matter of fact, I have." Then she grew sober. "That is, I had. We don't know whether he is still alive or not." She sighed. "He was seized on the pretext of his having smuggled arms into Israel, and his house in Tel Aviv was destroyed. That was three months ago and we haven't heard a word since. His daughter is working now as a practical nurse in the Tel Aviv hospital. Even she cannot find out any news about him. He has just disappeared. They're afraid it is an Arab reprisal for some shooting that was done by fanatics along the border."

Bill's eyes were blazing with interest.

"You have many relatives in Israel?"

"Yes, but only one whom I have ever seen. My cousin Yehudi was in this country a short time on—" she caught herself, "on business."

Bill did not miss the slip but he made no reference to it.

Rose had forgotten her embarrassment. It was plain to be seen that the subject of her Israeli relatives was close to her heart.

"My uncle was a prominent leader," she reminisced, "so my mother tells us, in the great Israeli stand for independence in 1948. It is probable, they think, that is why he has been seized again. The Arabs are afraid of him."

"There are great leaders among your people. In fact, I believe Israel is the key to the whole world situation." There was deep respect in his tone.

The lobster appeared just then and the conversation

77

was interrupted. Once more Rose tried to revert to commonplaces.

"This is a delightful place," she said, taking in the tasteful colors and the few really fine wall paintings.

"Yes, I like it," agreed Bill. "I found it by accident one day when I had to stop for some work on my car out on the highway. There isn't another restaurant within miles. It is run by two old maiden ladies. It was originally their own home. I believe they still live upstairs. Most of the house is furnished with handsome antiques. I hear that one of the sisters does most of the cooking herself."

"It's strange, isn't it," mused Rose, "how things change for people—for all of us, I suppose, although I haven't lived long enough to see much of it happen to me. Have you?" she added the question quite on the spur of the moment.

Bill was a long time answering.

"Yes, I have," he replied at last. "Quite a bit." Then he flashed a joyous smile at her. "It has been a terrific change, meeting you! I think it has been *almost* the most important change in my life." He was so sober that Rose started to ask what he meant by "almost." Then suddenly she thought she knew, and changed the subject.

They lingered over dessert until Rose looked at her watch.

"Oh, I must fly!" she exclaimed. "I'm supposed to be on duty for Mrs. Ross in ten minutes. I had no idea the time had passed so quickly."

"We'll make it," grinned Bill. "If you really don't mind flying. It's just nine miles, and the speed limit is 60 at night."

Rose noticed, with some amazement, that Bill left a ten dollar tip beside his plate. Was the boy reckless, or was he a millionaire?

CHAPTER 8

"I hate them for it!" The voice was frenzied, choked with bitterness. Rose stopped with her hand on the doorknob of Mrs. Ross's living room. It was a week or so after her dinner with Bill, and she had just come in, radiant, from a chat with him for a few minutes under the campus elms.

"They could have let me know. They let me go right on writing to him. I even sent him a little present. I— I wondered why he never wrote me a thank-you letter. It wasn't like him. Oh-h-h! He was such a sweet kid. But they *didn't like him.*"

Mrs. Ross's soft tones could be heard soothing the girl. Rose noiselessly opened the door a crack to let the housemother know she was on duty. There was Verna, sitting bolt upright in Mrs. Ross's straight desk chair, her mouth drawn up into a tight hard little purse, her eyes swollen with tears she would not shed. She was twisting her handkerchief as if she would take all her bitterness out on it.

"Come in, Rose," beckoned Mrs. Ross. "Verna has had a terrible shock. It will do her good to talk to you." She moved across the room awkwardly, whispering to Rose as she passed her, "She needs a lot of loving."

Rose was aghast. How could she go about comforting? Her own heart was too full of happiness. It was a shock to come from such bright thoughts straight into sorrow. She stood still, uncertain how to proceed. Verna seemed to pay no attention to either of them. Her face was contorted with fierce resentment.

The housemother soon realized that her helper was out of her depth. She drew a chair for herself near to

79

Verna and took one of her hands, gently stroking it. This strange child accepted sympathy with difficulty. She was evidently not used to expressions of affection.

"It's her little brother," explained Mrs. Ross. Thinking it might do the young freshman good to pour it out, she added to Verna, "You tell her, dear."

Verna cast a look of horror and despair at the woman and stood up.

"I'll never mention it again as long as I live. They were so afraid I'd get away from God," she scoffed. "Well, I have! And I'll never go home again." She marched savagely out of the room, her back as straight as a ramrod and her head high.

The two older women gazed after her helplessly. Mrs. Ross shook her head sadly. "She has been here for an hour," she said. "A letter came for her in the afternoon mail which she didn't get until after dinner. It was from one of her brothers. It seems that her little brother, of whom she was evidently very fond, was run over by the farm machinery and killed the day after she arrived here at college. The family didn't let her know until now. Her brother said her father didn't want her to spend money foolishly to come home, that there was no need, for she couldn't do anything, so he didn't tell her. That was nearly a month ago. The poor girl is beside herself with grief and shock. I can scarcely blame her. It must be a strange family that would even consider not letting her know. She has turned against all of them. My heart aches for her. I can't understand her mother allowing it."

Rose had dropped down in a big chair in dismay. It was inconceivable to her that a family could be so callous.

"You mean they did that just for fear of her spending the carfare?"

"That's what she says. She's going to need a great deal of attention and love or she may become a mental case."

"That's for sure. I would myself. How would one meet a thing like that without going completely berserk?"

Suddenly Rose wished she hadn't asked that question.

"Oh, I know, you're going to say by prayer or something like that." She looked quizzically, wistfully at Mrs. Ross, who smiled good-humoredly back at her.

"If you already know, why ask?"

"I don't know, not really. Tell me. Is there a way to meet such a thing, except by plain old 'grin and bear it'? It seems to me a person could grin just so many times, and bear just so much and then he'd break."

"May I have permission," Mrs. Ross rallied her, "to quote Isaiah?"

Rose threw up her hands.

Mrs. Ross smiled, then quoted tenderly, "He was a man of sorrows, and acquainted with grief. Surely He hath borne *our* sorrows . . . ' It takes someone who has suffered to be able to comfort. Someone who knows because He has gone through the same thing. That is one reason why God became man."

"You mean Jesus Christ."

"Yes. Who else?"

Rose was silent.

"Didn't Moses write of Him? When God spoke of the sufferings of Israel in Egypt didn't He refer to Himself as 'I AM come down to deliver?' I AM is Jehovah, you know. Jesus Christ was always identifying Himself with Him; 'I am the way'; 'I am the truth;' 'I am the resurrection.' Did ever any other god come down himself to deliver man?"

"You make it all fit together and sound so reasonable. But maybe it's just that you see it that way."

"Your eyes will be opened, too, one of these days, darling." Mrs. Ross leaned over and kissed Rose gently on her forehead. "Now I'm going up to Verna."

"But you were going out tonight," exclaimed Rose.

"And I was late and held you up. I ought to be able to stay with Verna," she said anxiously, "but I just don't know how."

"Of course not, dear. I don't need to go out anyway tonight. Verna needs someone with her to love her. I'm afraid her roommate won't understand."

"That icicle? No, that's for sure."

Mrs. Ross smiled and limped out.

Rose found herself sitting again where she had been that afternoon a week ago, with the same old problem facing her. She was no nearer to its solution, but she knew that she was much nearer to knowing what the root of the problem was, and it terrified her. *What* would she do with Jesus? More and more she realized that she would have to do something. Either reject and repudiate all that Mrs. Ross meant in her life, or admit that what Mrs. Ross said was true and that would have to mean going along with it all, one hundred percent. The frightful cost of that floored her.

The sudden discovery that she had nothing in her to meet the need of a young person like Verna was something of a shock. Perhaps she wasn't old enough, she argued with herself. But she knew very well that her lack was not age or experience. It was something that Mrs. Ross had that made her different from anyone Rose had ever known—except, maybe, Bill! Bill was certainly different, and he was very little older than she. He must know something of what Mrs. Ross was talking about or he never could have given that astonishing report in political science class. Somehow the brightness of her evening was dimmed. Perhaps the thing that these two people had was not for her. Anyway, she was tired and puzzled. Another time she would take it out and try to find the answer.

The phone rang. It was Sam.

"I have a letter from—guess who?"

Rose caught her breath. From the tone of his voice she knew. "Yehudi?"

"Right. Are you free? I could come over now and let you read it. There's news—real news. I'll see you."

Rose waited in a whirl of wonder. When Sam thrust the letter into her hands the words scarcely made sense to her. Some jumped out from the page and others sank away to a blank. She had already guessed what the news would be, and in spite of having been brought up all her life to hope, pray and expect the miracle to happen, now, alarmingly, she found a strange dread lest it had.

. . . and Ben Gurion has finally agreed to double the offer to the Arab republic. It is assumed by both sides here that the deal will go through. After two thousand years Mt. Zion will be ours! Israel's temple worship will be restored! To think that it is *our* privilege to live in the generation that brings these things about. Our people here have worked and have given; it is not enough. Do urge every Jew you know to give as never before. And if there are any willing to work, and fight as they work, plead with them to come and help us. Tell Sam to use his writing talent to issue a call to Jewry everywhere. Spare no effort. As you know, the materials for the Temple are prepared. The building itself could be erected in a short time—perhaps for Rosh Hashanah. Can't you hear the sound of the silver trumpet calling us all to worship? Think of Israel having her Temple again! My heart nearly bursts when I think of it.

Of course there are many problems yet to be ironed out. But if God has permitted us to progress this far, surely He will perform that which He has begun, according to the word of the prophets.

There was more; the letter was long. The brother and sister were accustomed to Yehudi's ecstasies, but now their own eyes were shining; they had scarcely dared believe that this thing would ever come to pass. From childhood they had grown accustomed to the thought of centuries of waiting. They had heard the matter discussed at home and at the synagogue.

83

"Did he write the news home, too?" asked Rose, thinking of what this would mean to their parents.

"Yes, the letter was originally to them. See? 'Dear Uncle Harry.' Dad sent it right on to us. Rose," Sam looked thoughtful, "I wonder whether I should stay here? Perhaps I could be more useful over there."

Rose pondered a while. "I don't see how," she finally decided. "They need trained men; you aren't ready yet. Oh, Sam, you should never have started me off first. I should never have allowed it."

"Hush up, Rosie. I'll never be sorry. Look at how you have made good. You've earned a scholarship. I'm the one who costs money. I'd like to quit right now and go back to work. It will take every cent we all can earn for the fund." He spoke almost feverishly.

"I feel that way, too, but don't forget that Israel will need trained workers. We can turn in what we have now, and go on to make ourselves worth more. I'll have a few dollars to give." She smiled. "It's time for me to get my hair cut again."

"I hate to see you do it, Rose. But I almost wish I could let mine grow if I could get anything for it." They both laughed.

"What a beatnik you'd make! But mine will grow again," Rose assured him. "I'm glad it grows fast. It's little enough I get for it, but it all helps."

They talked on, between interruptions for Rose's services.

"Sam, I'm worried about that Verna girl you told me to look up."

"Yeah?" responded Sam with mild interest.

"She was in here tonight with Mrs. Ross. Don't let this get around—it wouldn't be fair to her—but she's had a terrible blow." She told her brother in a few words about the letter Verna had received.

He whistled. "Say, that's really tough!" They were both silent a few moments trying to imagine themselves in a similar situation. "That is plain lowdown," decided Sam. "Enough to throw most kids. VeeEm has what it takes, I believe. There's something about that girl, square though she is, that you have to admire." He described again how she had stood up that day in class in response to Mr. Karpen's ribald invitation. "She doesn't know what the score is most of the time, but she's in the game. I don't dig that kind of fanaticism but you've got to hand it to her. If someone would take her in hand they could do something with her. Why don't you try, sis?"

"Me?" gasped Rose. "Why, I couldn't get to first base with her. Mrs. Ross asked her to talk to me and she froze and said she would never mention the whole thing again. She vows she isn't ever going home again either."

Sam raised pitying eyebrows. "Can't say as I blame her. S'pose our folks done that to one of us! I can't picture it. But say, Rosie, there's your chance. If she won't go home why don't you invite her to spend Thanksgiving holidays with us?"

Rose shot a curious teasing glance at her brother. Could it be that he had fallen for the little Dutch girl?

Sam caught the look and sputtered. "Don't go getting notions. No, I don't care whether I ever see her again, but I think it's only right to be human. The kid is all mixed up."

Rose sighed. "Yes," she agreed. "But I don't know but I'm just as mixed up myself."

"Yeah? What gives?"

But Rose simply shrugged and said nothing. How could she explain the strange yearning that gnawed at her heart day and night?

In Edward Karpen's little office, Edda Wittig, Colley Corbett and three or four other students were gathered, for a "workshop" Karpen called it when he gave the invitation through Edda.

"There are actually only a few who are equipped for

85

the study of political science," he explained to the little gathering. "In today's educational milieu there is increasing emphasis upon going the second mile with the gifted—a pity that there are so few really gifted in the science of government and governmental thinking. Politics has not yet been accepted as an exact science. But we must beware lest we limit ourselves and choke progress.

"I do not think I flatter myself when I say that after some years of observation in my classrooms, I am fairly well qualified to pin-point those in my classes who are so gifted, with whom it is worth my while to spend more time than the small amount doled out by an administration not always as enlightened as it might be."

He tucked his small hands into his trouser pockets and flung a charming smile about on the little company. Besides Edda, who wore the air of being hostess to the rest, and Corbett, who was desperately trying to conceal his boredom in order to preserve his scholastic standing, there were two young men whose haircuts and slovenly dress proclaimed them of beatnik status; a wide-eyed freshman girl with an eager beaver look, and two fellows who could be counted on to bring up questions in class.

"I believe in this little group gathered here!" Karpen spoke with holy fervor which set them all on pedestals. "If only you can catch the vision of what America can be; if you can condition yourselves to adjust to the changes that must come if there is to be growth instead of stagnation, believe me, young people, there is nothing, *nothing* that can stand in your way." He leaned forward and seemed to draw them to him in his earnestness. The man had an almost hypnotic charm at times. "You can develop into a power that can sway the thoughts and actions of this whole institution—yes, even the entire educational world, and you know *what that means!* The boundaries are nothing short of the universe itself. Think of the possibilities of Tomorrow!"

Jane Meecham, the eager beaver, was listening in dewy-eyed wonder. There was a magnetic resonance in the man's voice that held the attention of even Colley Corbett. The near beatniks snapped their fingers softly in time to the nodding of their unbarbered heads. Edda sat straight and assured; this was the path to Power, and Power was her dish.

One of the questioners, a bullet-headed fellow named Posden, spoke up. "You mean, sir, what you mentioned in class today—the carrying out of a project chosen by the group itself?"

"It would definitely be a group enterprise, conceived by the group, planned by the group, and carried out by the group. Of course to accomplish this each must be prepared to condition himself to change. Remember that change is the essence of progress."

"What shall be our project?" naively put in Jane.

"Ah! That will be for the group to decide, at our next meeting. Be thinking! Nothing is beyond the power of the group mind!"

There were further questions, vague answers, and some discussion; then the meeting adjourned until the next week.

"We'll keep our group small, for easy handling, but there is no objection to your inviting a few friends, if you like," was Karpen's parting charge. "Only choose them wisely. I can trust your judgment, I'm sure." He smiled; they were flattered. "In time, of course, we shall expand to—who knows?" He waved his arms to take in the college, the country, and possibly outer space.

Edda returned to the dorm to find her roommate struggling with fierce determination, to arrange her hair in the ear buns that Edda had achieved before.

Verna had refused to talk to Mrs. Ross. To all her loving advances the girl had remained stolid. It was as if she had suddenly turned to cold steel. At last Mrs. Ross sadly gave up.

Edda had set her mental wheels in motion as soon as she left Karpen's office. To her it was quite in line with her own masterful planning that she should find Verna already plowed and cultivated by some unknown husbandman so that she was prepared for Edda's new seed to be sown. She had never seen her new young partner in such a reckless, rebellious mood.

"How do you make it stay?" snapped Verna with an exasperated sigh.

"Here, put your bobby pins in the other way and cross one over the other," Edda deftly managed the bun.

"Oh dear!" cried Verna. "Why can't I make it look like that? I've worked and worked on it."

Edda gave a superior little smile. This was progress. If she could get this child to eating out of her hand, there was potential in her that would enhance Edda's own sense of power, and it could be used. "Oh, you'll get it in time. You've never worked with your looks much, have you?"

Verna flushed and then set her lips. "No. I don't know how." Then she whirled in her chair to face Edda. "Would you show me?" Her pitiful pleading attitude would have softened some girls. Edda felt only pride in having cleared her first hurdle.

"Sure," she agreed carelessly. "But if you want your square corners off you'll have to do as I say."

Verna thought a moment.

"That's funny," she said, "That's what Sam said to me the first day I came. I mean about square corners. I wasn't sure what he meant. I think I am beginning to understand." She hesitated a long moment then she took a deep, determined breath. "All right. I'm ready. What do I do?"

"Sam?" Edda spoke with a sneer. She was putting polish on her nails; she stopped. Hate twisted her features. The humiliating squelch Sam had given her in the political science class still rankled. Edda never forgot. To have him show attention to a country Dutch square was more than she could take without striking back. Edda was not impulsive, however; she always laid her plans carefully and she was willing to wait. A propitious time would arrive.

"Oh. Isn't he the 'son of Abraham' "—her tone was indescribable—"that made such an idiot of himself in political science class? And by the way, you ask what to do? For one thing, drop the religious bit. It's putrid!"

Verna felt herself freezing inside; she quickly got up and walked toward the clothes closet. She wanted to slip inside and never come out. She longed to hide her head in the lap of the dresses hanging there, the only soft things, it seemed, in a world turned frighteningly hard. She resented Edda's jab at Sam. Not only that, but the one thing she had been brought up to hold sacred, to cherish at all costs, to hang onto till her last breath lest some unnamed, unvisualized calamity take place, that thing she was being forced to abandon—or lose what she now found she wanted more than life itself, something that to her *was* life itself.

In her indecision she was torn. She had never known such agony. It was as if she were dying. It was even worse than the shock that had come in her brother's letter. The bitterness of that, dimmed for an hour while she sought escape in trivia, returned in full force now and mocked her. Those who had taught her ideals and held her to them with a tenacity that fairly choked the life out of her, had turned out to be heartless and unloving. What was there to hold to? Didn't it prove that all their talk of faith in God was a mere front?

Suddenly she whirled and faced Edda.

"All right." Her voice was tight and tense. "I will. Now what next?"

Edda laughed, a hard triumphant little laugh. She rose and put away her manicuring tools and switched out her light. "Don't rush me. There's plenty of time. My old nurse used to say, 'There's all tomorrow ain't been touched yet.' "

89

But Verna, struggling in the passion of abandoning her old self, was not satisfied. She could not sleep. She wanted action; denied that, she must have something to help her forget. She flung off her clothes, slanted her reading light away from Edda's eyes and plunged into calculus. If she was to try to keep up with Edda, who had gradually become to her inexperienced vision all that represented security and power, she must excel in every field. The nearest and easiest field for her, was the academic. She *must* beat Edda at her own game. Edda was smart, but Verna would be smarter. Beneath her awe of the older girl, she was unaware of a deep resentment amounting almost to hatred. The feeling was still all but smothered by her sense of need—need of being rescued from a slough of obscurity and inferiority. Edda herself, unfortunately, was the only one available to help.

For hours Verna wrestled with her lessons. The turmoil in her mind was too great for her usual concentration. She would read over a whole page and then couldn't recall a single thought in it. It was her grandmother's warning that harassed her now. Several times she turned out the light and decided to go to sleep and study in the morning. But sleep would not come. Then she would start in on the books again. It was nearly four o'clock before she fell into a troubled doze, and thought that her father and Edda were Roman soldiers dragging her brother Richard and her away to the arena to be torn by lions. Just as they reached the entrance, there was Sam offering to rescue them, but Edda only gave a mocking laugh and kicked him aside. Verna tried to cry out to God for help, but He called back that it was no use, for she had denied Him. The lions seized Richard and she awoke screaming.

Her nightmares roused Edda, who routed her out pettishly and made her get up since it was morning anyway.

"You're going to have to do something about those

impossible clodhoppers you wear," commanded Edda gazing with undisguised loathing at the sturdy, sensible brown oxfords her roommate was tying. "Talk about square!"

Verna raised her eyes in dismay. "Oh!" Suddenly the shoes became spectres of deformity. "But how can I?" she wailed. "I don't have the money."

Edda shrugged. "That's your worry. You wanted me to tell you."

"Yes," agreed Verna and sighed. Could any human being feel more degraded than she at this moment? She felt like tearing off the offending footwear and going barefoot. She had no other shoes, except a black pair just like these.

"Get some flats," argued Edda. "Even thongs would be better than those. But flats don't cost very much; two or three bucks, maybe."

Edda had no idea what a huge sum two or three dollars appeared to the girl who was brought up never to waste a nickel, to say nothing of a dollar. Verna knew just what her father would say: "You *got* shoes, ain't? Then *wear* 'em a'ready." But that was the father who had hidden from a loving sister the terrible tragedy of his own son's death, all for the sake of a five-dollar carfare. Something in Verna sensed the criminality of it, though she could not have put it into words. In her present state of mind anything at all that savored of her father's precepts was anathema.

"I'll get them," she replied with meek resolve. "Ugh! I hate to put these on again even to go to breakfast."

Edda gave a sardonic chuckle. "What size do you wear? Eights? Try these." She flung a pair of red ballet slippers across to where Verna sat on the edge of her bed. The Dutch girl gasped.

"Oh! No!" she recoiled. "Uh——they're yours! I couldn't do that."

Edda burst out again with a jeering snicker. "Why

91

don't you say what you mean? You haven't the nerve to wear those red ones!" She rocked with laughter.

Stung by the taunt, Verna retorted, "Oh, it isn't that. It's just that I can't take yours. I—I might ruin them." But her very tone of voice proved that she was covering up, that Edda had hit her weak spot.

"Ruin those things! So what?" shrugged Edda giving a final spray to her slinky hairdo.

"Come on, get into them and let me fix your hair. Make it snappy. I can't wait all morning; I'm starved."

As they walked over to the dining room, the very first time that Edda had condescended to go with her roommate, Verna caught sight of herself, as of a stranger, in the full length mirror at the head of the stairs. The glimpse fairly took her breath. She had to admit that she looked more like other girls. The style of her hair was pertly becoming to her, and her feet seemed almost to dance along in the light little kid shoes, like a leprechaun's.

Her spirits rose; she felt gay, more lighthearted than she had ever felt in all her life. Then like the slam of a heavy door came the recollection of that letter yesterday and all that had followed. Her heart went down like a lead weight on the end of a broken rope. And there was nothing left with which to haul it up again. Verna set her round jaw. All right, she'd go on anyway, in her own way, the path of her own choice. Family standards should have no more influence on her, she decided. And she'd show these people here that she was not "square."

She took her place in the breakfast line with her head high and a forced gay laugh on her lips. Sam saw her and raised his brows in mild astonishment. Rose saw her and frowned in troubled wonder. And Colley Corbett saw her for the first time, as it were, since college opened.

CHAPTER 9

The political science classes continued to be a source of debate amounting at times to dissension. Edward Karpen was a past master at stirring up discussion. All he had to do was to fling one small bone to the pack and they were all at it tooth and nail.

"The question at issue today is whether we want the traditional form of government which benefited the limited few, or a government for all.

"Are you going to go right on swallowing all the conventional hokum that has been dealt out like pablum to babies for so many years, or are you going to blaze the way for new frontiers, new concepts, a whole new framework to open up the new space age? We need a new world leader for the new 'one world.' It could be one of you!"

These were typical questions that he used to start the class, and they never failed to bring the desired result. When the students found that high grades went to talkers who imitated his line of argument, they talked. But those few who were original enough to do their own thinking were also wise enough to examine his catch phrases and be disturbed.

When he wanted to liven up a particularly dull session Karpen would always turn to religion.

Bill rarely spoke except when questioned directly. Even Karpen's favorite challenge: "Is your viewpoint on religion your own, or is it a tradition handed down from your fathers?" failed to stir Bill, although many another student was set to thinking.

Among the latter were Sam and Verna.

After class one day, Sam noticed Verna just ahead in the corridor. Her amber hair, in buns now every

93

day as a matter of course, never failed to attract his attention. He caught up with her.

"How's it goin', VeeEm?" he accosted her gaily.

Ever since her first day at college his voice had always made something leap inside of her. She was perfectly well aware that his friendliness was bestowed on all alike, that it was not just for her, but somehow that first short hour of confidences, when he had seemed to read her misery and know just how to meet it for her, had been set apart in her own heart as something special that she would treasure all her life. It was probably the only time a young man had ever treated her as a flesh and blood human girl.

She flashed him an astonished smile. She didn't know that Sam was noticing with pleasure what an attractive, wide smile she had, and how white and even were her teeth. She no longer expected him to pay much attention to her. That day on the bus riding up to the college—what an innocent she had been! When he left her so summarily she had been just a little bit hurt. But in the light of even the small measure of sophistication that was now hers she realized that his place then had been with the fellows. How she had learned that she could not fathom. But she took courage because she had learned it.

"I am pretty well—considering." She hadn't yet adopted the current lingo. Slang catch phrases were not ready to her tongue. She still spoke with a soft, prim, painstaking correctness that she had worked so hard to develop under the tutelage of her excellent English teacher at high school.

Sam liked the purity of her English speech; it was a refreshing change from the current, clipped flippancy.

But he noticed the tinge of bitterness in her tone.

"Got a class next period?" he asked casually.

"No, no more today."

"Let's leave our books here on the rack and hike off a bit, okay?"

Surprised and pleased, she assented.

He touched her arm lightly, guiding her through the crowd of students hurrying here and there. It was the first bit of personal chivalry that had come her way and it stirred her deeply. She had noted how the fellows whom she characterized as the nicer ones performed little courteous acts for their girls. Some boys, of course, were crude, like her own brothers; they were not the ones she admired. She was glad that Sam was of "the cream," as she put it.

They took the path that hundreds of couples had taken before them, the way that led through the woods back of the dorm and up to the top of the hill. The trees were beginning to display their exciting new fall colors. The heat had given way to an anticipatory crispness in the air. Late summer insects already sounded as if they were too drowsy to do efficient buzzing. The air was clear, sunny, and restful. Part of the pathway was padded with pine needles; the scent was exhilarating.

When they reached the flat rock they stood awhile breathing in the artless splendor flung out across hill and valley.

"Do you like thunderstorms?" In all seriousness Verna asked the question. The apparent incongruity of it startled Sam. Was this strange girl deeper than she appeared or merely erratic? That she was not making an attempt to impress him by eccentricity was evident. She was utterly sincere. Unless he answered in kind she would be hurt. She was utterly trusting him to meet her mind.

"Yes, why?" He did not smile as if she had said something odd.

"I was just thinking," she said musingly, "that this is so beautiful it almost hurts to take it in, yet if we were here in a terrific storm it would be just as gorgeous, only in a different way."

"I guess you're right," he agreed thoughtfully. "I don't know that I ever thought of it like that."

"Well," she went on, unselfconscious for the first time since she left home, "who is to say that a purply black sky with zig-zag gold streaks shooting through it isn't just as artistic as blue with this shimmery gold light all over it?"

She turned wide, amber eyes upon him in ingenuous confidence that he would accept her evaluations without surprise or ridicule. He was suddenly grateful that he could measure up, that he did understand her, that from somewhere in his heritage he had received the ability to think beyond the surface of the things that are seen. It had actually never occurred to him before that he did think more deeply than most young persons. In the startling discovery of another's perceptiveness, he knew it to be so in himself. His first impulse had been to banter her with some typical cliché like, "You must be an art major." But by some untapped source of wisdom he was aware that that would effectively and instantly dam the tide of her personality which she was pouring out before him so innocently and prodigally. This was what the poor child had needed, an understanding ear. She had had none at home, perhaps, in all her life. And who was there here to listen? Frustration was her difficulty. Perhaps he was the one to cure her. "But why me?" he dodged. "What's the matter with her housemother? Or the guidance counselor? I'm too busy to take on a psychiatric case, and besides I don't know enough about it. I'm not trained for that sort of thing!" Nevertheless, the need was present now, and he surprised himself by saying,

"Perhaps it's because the same God made both. They say connoisseurs can spot the work of certain artists by their special characteristics. There is no artist like Him."

Slowly Verna turned again that wondering look on him.

"Then you know God!" There was vast relief in her voice.

"Well," he shied, "I don't know that I'd go so far as to say that. I wish I did. But I know something *about* Him. I believe there's a difference. Anyway, I don't go along with the rubbish that political science fellow is heaving at us. That's for the birds." They sat on the stone bench and he selected a long pine needle from those scattered about and began to chew the end of it.

Verna gazed off at the hills. "My roommate thinks he's wonderful."

"She's that long drink of water with the mermaid eyes, isn't she?"

Verna gave a disappointed laugh. "Is that the way she seems to you? I thought she was considered very stylish. At least she thinks—Oh! I shouldn't say that. She has really been very kind to me lately. She's helping me—what was it you said that first day—to 'rub the corners off'?"

Sam laughed. "I guess I was pretty hard on you."

"No." She spoke with certainty. "I needed it. I can see a little of what you meant. But it hasn't been exactly pleasant."

"But your roommate is not so bad after all? I recall she was your *bête noire* the last time we talked."

"No, she's probably kind at heart. But I never could talk to her as we are talking now. For one thing, she told me I had to give up my religion if she was going to help me. She called it 'putrid.'"

"Yeah?" Sam waited. "And what did you say to that?"

Verna didn't answer for quite a while. Sam went on chewing the pine needle, threw it away and chose a fresh one. At last she said in a shamed voice, "I told her I would."

Sam turned quickly to look at her. He was obviously surprised.

She met his gaze and dropped her eyes. "You didn't

think I would, did you? Not after I stood up in class that day. Well, I saw how foolish that was. I knew after I did it that that wasn't what we were supposed to do. I felt like a silly fool."

"I didn't think you were a silly fool," Sam said. "Suppose it wasn't what the guy wanted—you really threw a wrench into his performance. It did him good —and me too. I thought you were swell. No one else was brave enough to do it."

"*You* did."

"Oh, not exactly. I told him off in a way. I figured we were wasting time. I was burned up for Bill. He's a swell fellow."

"Who is he? I notice he doesn't do a lot of talking in class."

"He's a roommate of mine. A real guy. I don't always agree with him, but he's okay. Comes from New York. He sure is different. He's had a lot of trouble. Maybe that's what makes him seem so much older, and sort of dependable."

"Have you had a lot of trouble?"

"Me? Oh, I don't think I've had more than the ordinary fellow's share. Why?"

"You seem older and dependable."

"Do I? Well, thanks for that. I don't feel so. There are lots of things I don't feel sure of at all."

"Me too. I used to think there were things—people —you could count on."

Sam waited. It would do her good if she would talk about the death of her brother, but he couldn't let her know that he had heard of it. That would betray Rose's confidence. But Verna told no more, only sighed heavily.

Finally she said, "I've analyzed what Mr. Karpen said about religion. I've decided I'm the way he said, that all I have is just what I sort of inherited. I don't really know God first hand, for myself." She sighed again, wistfully this time.

Sam waited, chewing his pine needle. "Could be," he said laconically.

Finally she rose. "I guess I ought to be getting back," she said. "It has been nice," she added.

"Yes, I've enjoyed it," agreed Sam and realized that it was true. "We'll have to try it again sometime."

She brightened. "Oh, I'd love that!"

"Maybe there will be a good thunderstorm next time," he laughed.

He left her at Holley Hall. She thanked him again with quaint old-fashioned courtesy and never knew that it was quaint or old-fashioned.

Mama would like her, thought Sam casually as he turned away.

Verna went upstairs with a lighter heart. Why was it that she always felt more at peace after talking to Sam?

She was surprised to find a note from Edda in her room: "Hunt me up in the library. Don't plan anything for tonight."

Verna could scarcely believe her eyes. It fairly took her breath to think that the girl she had considered so mean and unfriendly actually cared to have her get in touch and perhaps was planning a pleasant time for her tonight—or was she? A few weeks ago Verna would have suspected that Edda only wanted her to do an unpleasant errand for her. But the whole atmosphere had changed amazingly. What had caused it? She was humble enough to believe that it was she herself who had been the unconscious fly in the ointment. Now that she gave evidence of change herself, others were more ready to be friendly. That must be it.

Thrilled to think that she had someone who wanted to see her, just like other girls with pals, she raced over to the library, expecting to find the same warmth that the note had indicated.

Edda was in the student lounge outside the library proper, her long slim legs crossed, accentuating the tightness of her pencil slim skirt, writing mysterious notes back and forth with Tracy Posden. She scarcely glanced up when Verna rushed breathlessly in.

"What is it, Edda?" whispered Verna excitedly.

Edda was slow to raise her eyes. Then the coolest of glances passed over her roommate, and she curled her lip. "Get lost!" was all she said. Then she turned away and gave all her attention to reading Posden's note.

Verna waited, uncertain. At last it dawned upon her that Edda had no intention of speaking further to her and awkwardly she went out, mortified. By the time she reached her room she was furious with Edda. She *was* mean, after all. She had merely wanted to embarrass her. Now if she did have any nice plan for the evening, Verna was not sure she would want to join in it. In angry frustration she seized her books and plunged again into study. More than ever she meant to humiliate Edda. She was her classmate in three courses. She would top her grades in every one and make a higher overall grade point record, besides. Exams were due next week. She determined to let nothing, absolutely nothing deter her from her purpose.

It was Thursday, the day that Verna had always made sure to get a letter off to her family. The thought occurred to her, but she set her lips in a bitter line and opened her textbook instead.

When Edda came in, just in time to freshen up for dinner, Verna was prepared to give her as cool a shoulder as she had presented to her. But Edda was all smiles. She paid no attention to Verna's preoccupation; she chattered excitedly while she hurried into clean clothes.

"You're to go with us tonight to Mr. Karpen's workshop; isn't that a break? He doesn't let everyone come, you know. It's a sort of political science club, really; something like the Spanish club and the French club. It was just started a week or two ago, for those who

100

he says have some ability in political science. He told us that we knew the rest of the class better than he, and perhaps some other students would appreciate it. So we were each to invite someone. Of course just to be in it will probably rate us an A for interest. And I know how serious you are and what a good student and all that, so I put your name in and he's okayed it. Isn't that simply terrific? You're made with him if you go for his line, and of course I do think he's simply marvelous when he gets to talking on world problems. I could listen to him all night. He has such an intellectual manner and his eyes are divine. Now you are to wear this red jersey of mine tonight, and the red flats, and let me do your hair. You're getting on to doing it but we want it just right for tonight. You *may* pick up a date. Guess what I heard Colley Corbett say about you! No, I'm not going to tell you, maybe he'll tell you himself. But he certainly has had his eye on you ever since you began to act more like a human being."

Verna listened with amazement, her head still bent over her book. Pleased as she was over Edda's praise, and enticing as the plan sounded, she was not one to forget so easily the rebuff in the library lounge.

She faced Edda.

"Tell me why you treated me as you did in the library."

"Oh, that!" Edda's very tone of voice brushed the incident away as if it had been a wisp of smoke. "You'll learn some day, my dear, that you simply don't interrupt when a girl is talking to a fellow."

"But your note *said* to——"

"How did I know there would be a man waiting there to talk to? Now come here and try this on. Make it snappy."

In spite of herself, Verna obeyed. She might lose all the ground she had gained if she didn't.

CHAPTER 10

At dinner Colley Corbett and Tracy Posden brought their trays to the girls' table and sat down.

Colley always attracted girls wherever he was. His broad shoulders and his confident swagger made him in some eyes very desirable. Verna had not classed him in her mind with those she considered "cream." But it did feel pleasant to have a popular young man at her side looking at her so admiringly.

"Sharp tonight, aren't you?" he began boldly. "I s'pose you have a name, but I forget it." He laughed as if, seeing that his own was Colley Corbett, other people's names didn't matter.

"Call me VeeEm," responded Verna trying to sound as flip as other girls she had heard conversing with boys. As soon as she said the name, she was sorry she had used it, for somehow it belonged especially to Sam. It was connected with the time he had come so wonderfully to her rescue; she still treasured that memory. Nevertheless, she was ashamed to give her real name. She knew by now that it would provoke only jeers.

Edda and her friend Posden were discussing the meeting they were all to attend, and Verna withdrew from active conversation to listen. Anything that would give her a better grade, she was interested in.

"I wonder who else will be there tonight," ventured Posden.

"I think maybe my roommate will come," spoke up Corbett. "I invited him. I wanted some fun. If I have to put through the evening anyway, to get a passing grade, I might as well have some excitement out of it. You can count on Bill Lodge and old Karp to tangle."

"Bill Lodge!" exclaimed Verna impulsively. "He's Sam Goldman's roommate, isn't he?"

"Yes, old Bill puts up with us all, even Sam."

The two couples remained together after dinner and sauntered together to the club meeting.

Verna's eyes were bright. The red jersey dress was noticeable rather than becoming, since Edda was considerably slimmer than her roommate. If Verna had taken her usual glimpse in the full length mirror she might have demurred at appearing in it, but Edda had hustled her off without a chance to see how she looked. There were several raised eyebrows, wolf calls, and a snicker or two among both fellows and girls when the four entered the room. But Verna was oblivious of them. She felt secure at last in the approval of a stylish sophomore and the fact that she had a real date. She took her seat self-consciously and Colley placed his chair beside her. She looked around and recognized a few students she knew. Joan Denison was there, and Pinky Clapp. *What a lot I have learned,* thought Verna complacently, *since that first day on the train.*

Bill and Sam came in at the last minute and remained at the back of the room. They were out of the line of Verna's vision.

The subject for discussion was the selection of a project for the group to carry into effect.

"Remember," reminded Mr. Karpen in opening the meeting, "that whatever is accomplished here will be accomplished by you as a group. Individuals in the group will grow in sensitivity, in observation and in group leadership, but the main thing is that you keep in mind the group activity. Each individual will make his or her contribution to group thinking, but it is the group that will accept or reject what you contribute, on the basis of whether it furthers the group project. You see, we will be at grips with the basis of society; we shall see at first hand what makes society tick. You will together select a problem that needs to be solved,

103

and together you will consider the best means of solving it, and carry out that solution *by action of the group,* each losing himself, as it were, in the character of the group activity."

The company was more than twice the number that had attended the first gathering. Tacit promise of coveted A's drew some; curiosity brought others; Sam came because Bill did.

"You aren't going, are you?" questioned Sam in disgust after Colley had issued his invitation and left them one night.

Bill thought a few moments. "Yes, I believe I will." Sam showed his surprise but Bill did not explain.

As Mr. Karpen gave his introductory remarks the wide-eyed freshmen began to flounder. They had come with high hopes; but it began to sound like hard work; they might be required to think.

"Now remember," warned Mr. Karpen again, "we are here to pool our ideas creatively. You as a group must choose a project. I am not the leader. I am here only as a sort of clearing house. You, the group, are to lead yourselves."

There was a solemn, scared silence.

"In other words," spoke up one of the steady talkers, "we are all chiefs; there are no Indians." He giggled; his remark sounded rather smart to him. He was not quite sure whether that was the gist of Mr. Karpen's remarks, or whether it was a sort of mockery of his statements. It turned out to be the former. He heaved a sigh of relief.

"Exactly, Mr. Posden. This is to be a creative group. Actually you will be taking part in an experiment in group dynamics." He broke off and gave a pleasant little deprecatory laugh. "Does that sound too stiff for some of you? Never mind. You will find that you work into it naturally, because you are human beings. We shall be working with the stuff of human nature. That is what makes experiments like this so exciting. It's like a game. Now we must have a recording secretary, to take down a record of discussions so that we shall not waste time repeating ourselves. Mr. Posden, you seem interested. Does the group agree that Mr. Posden shall take over that work?"

No one dissented.

"Well, we must start somewhere, so let us just appoint him."

"Now how about an observer? As a group you will want a sort of mirror to reflect what your actions are, and show whether you are operating as a group. The observer can note whether the group spirit is present, or whether there may possibly be those who are uninterested or some who present isolated opinions. Let's see. Miss Wittig has done some little research in group dynamics and has discussed its methods with me. Suppose, Miss Wittig, that you take the position of observer. Does that please the group?"

Again no answer.

"Very well. Now, that starts us. I realize that this is all quite new to some of you. But all you will need is a little shove and off you'll go. Now for your project. Let the suggestions come from all of the group. Try to select a project that will be relevant to conditions right here among us. As you make your individual contributions see that you consider the group desires. I will simply guide you toward your goal. All ready with suggestions?"

Again there was silence. Mr. Karpen smiled understandingly.

"You still feel uncertain, don't you? Let me make some typical suggestions that have been used in other places. For instance, you might consider the question of on-campus rules, or the system of grading, or even such a widespread problem as the rights of students to intermarry among different races. How about raising or lowering standards of admission or graduation? Another problem is the voting age in this state; should it be lowered to include all high school graduates, or should it be raised so as to exclude those who have no college degree? Of course, those projects would be more difficult to carry out, but would not be impossible, given time and enthusiasm. Another area might be that of the methods of justice in the state; should the age limit of supreme court justices be lowered? Or perhaps we should consider working on more benefits for prisoners. How about a problem very close to home? Would it be wise to consider rotation of office here at the college so as to give every professor the right to have a part in the actual administration of the college? Perhaps that could be broadened to include also gifted seniors. You must begin to realize that you yourselves are a group with power; you have the potential to change existing conditions."

Suddenly Bill stood up.

"Sir," he boomed, "may I ask whether this meeting has the approval of the administration?"

"Ah!" exclaimed Mr. Karpen, as if delighted. "At last we are getting some reaction. Just as I hoped, there *is* creative thought among us. Suppose we rephrase Mr. Lodge's question so that it could very well become a real contribution to group thinking. It could be stated, project-wise, for discussion before we act on it: Should administration approval be necessary for informal group gatherings in the college? In fact, you could extend the problem to all informal group gatherings by college students during the school term, whether on or off the college grounds."

"That re-statement does not express my question, Mr. Karpen. I would like to repeat, does the administration sanction this meeting?"

"Well, now we have a good illustration right here in the group for you all to examine, of isolated thinking. Remember, young people, the goal you are striving for is we-centered thinking. Just let's not get off our course here. Thank you, Mr. Lodge, for your contribution.

Now, has anyone else a suggestion? Just follow along as a group. Use any one of those problems I gave you or better still, bring up one of your own. But remember!" He playfully extended a warning finger. "Keep your thinking we-centered." He gave another pleasant little laugh. "Come, someone else. Mr. Corbett, what do you have in mind?"

Colley cleared his throat impressively. Everyone's eyes were on him; he drew in his abdomen. But before he could come up with anything that remotely resembled an idea, Sam rose and stood beside Bill, who was still on his feet.

"It seems to me," he began in a tone seething with sarcasm, "that a most apt suggestion for this meeting would be whether or not this 'we-centered group' should amend the basic fundamentals of the constitution of the United States!"

He sat down, and Bill with him, muttering, "Bully for you, old man," under his breath.

Unperturbed, Mr. Karpen smiled again, condescendingly. "Well, of course amendments to the constitution have been achieved before, and probably will be again, but I admit that is a big undertaking for our first project. Perhaps we had better wait awhile for that. However, let the recorder take down all suggestions and we shall evaluate them at the end. You realize that we need not necessarily make our choice of a project at this particular meeting. But remember that the world is fast changing, and we must be prepared to change with it. Tomorrow, with all that it presages of progress or stagnation, will come all too swiftly."

"I'll say it will!" announced Bill clearly. A few chuckled, and low muttered remarks made about exams on the morrow.

Jane Meecham piped up. "I think your suggestion about lowering the standards for graduation would be a good one. It has always bothered me when I think of some students who try so very hard to get good grades,

107

but they have to drop out. It seems to me that something might be done for them."

"Well, what is the group thinking on that? Would it involve raising the standards of admission so that only the gifted were admitted in the first place?" Mr. Karpen looked around the room for discussion.

"Oh, my!" bleated Jane. "That would be worse than ever."

"But you see, there are many angles of a question to be considered. That is the very essence of group dynamics. Come now, all of you. Don't be afraid to express yourselves."

A voice here and there timidly mentioned one or the other of the subjects which Mr. Karpen had already listed. To each he gave smiling approval and called for more discussion. At last, after an hour of what seemed like aimless babbling, he called a halt.

"We have made some real progress tonight toward group dynamics. Some to whom this idea is new may not be able to evaluate yet, but in time you will see what has been accomplished. Now may we have a record read of our meeting and a brief summary of observations on the group attitudes."

Tracy Posden read a list of the suggestions by various ones; all of them were mere repetitions of Karpen's except Sam's which was recorded in all seriousness. No mention was made of Bill's challenge.

Edda welcomed the limelight. In a clear voice, in concise cutting phraseology, she stated that while the group as a whole had made progress in we-centered thinking, there were some who showed a tendency to cling to isolated ideas of their own instead of conforming to the group goal. Those members, she suggested, needed to evaluate their own need for adjustment to change.

After the meeting most of the young people crowded around Mr. Karpen, shaking his hand, thanking him for a wonderful evening, apologizing for being so stupid.

"But we'll catch on," they promised. "Don't you give us a grade yet. We'll get the idea before long."

He renewed his assurance of confidence in their group ability and smiled upon all.

Edda was in her glory. She talked fast and furiously. Several satellites orbited her.

Verna had not particularly enjoyed the meeting. Her mind was not in it. She had been more taken up with the new and not altogether pleasant experience of having a young man, in sight of all, paying rather noticeable attention to her. He laid his arm across the back of her chair, and more than once he let it slip down her arm when he turned to speak to someone behind him. The feeling it gave her was more akin to loathing than delight. Once he even looked down at her with a personalized grin and gave her a squeeze before he put his arm up again. Was this the sort of thing that girls liked on dates? It must be, for she had heard enough of their chatter now to recognize what was expected. She glanced down at herself. Early in the evening she had become aware of the tightness of the red dress; she squirmed a little to try to make more room for herself in it. But she was uneasy about it. Colley, she realized, was quite taken with it, giving meaningful glances here and there on her person. She was most uncomfortable.

It wasn't until Bill and Sam spoke out that she knew they were there. Her cheeks grew red to match her dress. Somehow she was aware that they would not approve of her looks tonight. Then she caught the note of challenge in Bill's speech, and that sarcasm in Sam's voice. She wished she had paid more attention to what Mr. Karpen had been saying. Something was the matter.

When she dared look toward the back of the room after the meeting broke up she couldn't locate either Bill or Sam. They must have gone out immediately. She was troubled.

But it was fun to saunter down to Lasky's afterwards, two couples together, and sit in the ice cream booth and listen and laugh. Verna even attempted a witty remark or two herself.

On the way home under the elms Colley slid his arm around her waist. She wished he wouldn't. But she could see the other couple ahead walking the same way. It must be the thing to do if you wanted friends.

"Where've you been all these weeks since school started?" joshed Colley. "You know what? You're way out, gal, in that outfit."

Verna gave an embarrassed, uncomprehending giggle. Since he spoke in a complimentary tone she deduced that "way out" must mean something nice. She tried to make conversation. She mentioned the meeting and managed to recall one or two phrases that had stayed with her.

"Oh, that rot?" was Colley's response. "Let the guy rave. He enjoys it. We don't have to do anything about it but be there. He's the kind that likes to hear himself talk, and give us an A for listening. Say, how about a show Saturday night?"

"A show?" Verna hesitated.

"Yeah. There's a good one down at the Grotto. Can you make it?"

Convinced that he was asking for a date, Verna panicked. This was what she had longed for but now that it had happened, she was frightened. Tonight had not been too difficult; she had simply followed Edda's lead. But alone? She wouldn't know how to manage.

"Why, I'll have to — see — if Edda — " Her voice trailed off.

"Oh, sure, if you want we can double date. We'll catch up and ask them. Hey there."

It was arranged, but Verna was still torn between ecstasy and terror.

"Well, that was a waste of time," spat out Sam.

The two young men had escaped from the meeting and were in the convertible again, taking a breather before going to bed.

"I'm not so sure," stated Bill soberly.

"You didn't enjoy it, certainly," gasped Sam. This new friend of his was so unpredictable.

"Hardly! But I think it's probably a good thing that we went. In fact, I believe I'll go again."

"Brother, you are a bear for punishment. I never was so bored. What a lot of tommyrot."

"Tommyrot, yes, but with a dose of poison in it. A lot of those kids were eating it up. They don't half think. To them he's the guy who can give good marks. They don't know that communism thrives on stuff like that. Whenever you hear all that tripe about change and progress, beware. Your crack about amending the constitution should have made them wise up, but did you notice how that clever character twisted it to sound plausible? He knew perfectly well that you were being sarcastic. The question is, how far does a thing like this have to go before it should be reported?"

"You don't think he really means to *do* anything about his crazy 'projects,' do you?"

"Could be. You said he had once refused to take a loyalty oath, didn't you?"

"If I'm right that he is Karpinsky."

"That can be proved, without too much difficulty, if it becomes necessary." Bill pulled the car over to the side of the road and stopped. "Look, Sam. Whether you know it or not, the whole world is at fever heat. And just like with pneumonia, or typhoid, the crisis is upon us. I meant what I said in that first report. There is a lot more to say. And it's not found merely in the New Testament, either. Your own prophets have made it so clear a fool oughtn't to miss it."

Bill was in dead earnest.

"Listen, fella," he went on. " 'It shall come to pass in that day — ' and you'll find that 'in that day' always refers to the time immediately preceding the next great judgment on the earth; the last one was the Flood — 'In that day the Lord shall set His hand again *the second time* to recover the remnant of His people . . .' — *the first time* was the Exodus — and He shall assemble the outcasts of Israel and gather together the dispersed of Judah . . . for the people shall dwell in Zion at Jerusalem.' See how the new state of Israel sets the clock for us? We are entering the time called 'that day.' Sam, that has happened. God kept His word and established your nation again in 1948, after nearly 2500 years."

Sam tried to think of a way to change the subject. He was embarrassed by his friend's intensity. "Yes, yes, I know it," he agreed. "But tell me, why are you interested in this?"

"Aren't you?"

"Yes, in a way. My cousin Yehudi thinks of nothing else, and we all have tried to help — a little."

But Bill persisted. "Why shouldn't everyone be interested? Haven't you read your own prophets? Ezekiel makes it very plain that there will be a confederacy of nations under Russia that will come down from the north and attack Israel 'in that day.'"

"Not again!" cried Sam with a groan.

"Yes, again. Details are given. There will also be a federation of nations something like NATO or the European Common Market, united together to combat the power of Russia. Oh, Sam, it is all there, so clear, just exactly what is beginning to take place today. The chariots jostling one another in the streets are mentioned; the pillars of smoke — could be from nuclear bombs; the changes in the heavens which our own scientists are fearful of right now because of nuclear power; the earth reeling 'to and fro like a drunkard'; war everywhere; demons loose on the earth; no place to hide from terror. The whole world is looking for a great world leader. He is described in the Bible —

112

a godless dictator who will demand worship. He will make a treaty with Israel allowing them to have their temple worship again. We can expect any time now that Israel will get possession of Mt. Zion and rebuild their temple — "

"Bill!" cried Sam. His voice held awe. "I want you to read a letter we got from my cousin. He says that Israel has doubled their offer and they expect to be able to buy Mt. Zion."

"No kidding!" exclaimed Bill eagerly. "Well, if some of the things prophesied have come to pass, why not all?"

It was Sam's turn to be excited. "Bill, I want to hear more of this. *Show* it to me. What does it all have to do with Karpen?"

"Well, there's no doubt in my mind that this Karpen fellow is one of Russia's stool pigeons. You can see that if Russia is aligned against the Western powers, and Israel is the prize that Russia wants, that there will be a terrific battle over Israel. And it's near. Listen: 'For behold, *in that day,* and *in that time,* when I shall bring again the captivity of Judah and Jerusalem, I will also gather all nations — that's a World War . . . and will bring them down into the valley of Jehoshaphat, and will plead with them there for my heritage Israel whom they have scattered among the nations.'"

Sam was scarcely breathing. He tried not to let Bill see how deeply he was stirred.

"'Multitudes, multitudes, in the valley of decision . . . the sun and the moon shall be darkened . . . the heavens and the earth shall shake . . . the day of the Lord is *near* in the valley of decision.' There is a lot more, Sam. I'm just giving you scraps that have stayed in my mind. But don't you see that this could all take place *tomorrow?* We are still this side of it, but for how long?"

Sam was still a long time. "I don't get it," he said at last, wonderingly, "that *you,* a Christian — we'd

113

call you a Gentile — know these things about Israel; and I, an Israelite, know nothing of them. *Why,* Bill? *Why?* My folks are good Jews. They have not departed from the faith as some have. Why don't they know it?"

Bill took an audacious leap. "Sam," he said gently, "when I tell you, I want to remember that I know that I am just a sinner like anyone else. I had to come to God by way of the blood sacrifice of Another, just as your people or any others must come. Never think I am judging your people. But this is what one of the greatest of your own leaders said long ago: 'Blindness in part is happened to Israel until the fulness of the Gentiles be come in.' I guess it's something like the way our puppy wouldn't eat his dinner until we called the cat to eat it; then the dog came running. God sent the truth to Israel first and when she turned from it and killed His prophets, and rejected His Son, God turned to the Gentiles to make Israel jealous enough to want His salvation. Now, because the Gentiles as a whole have not wanted His truth, either, it's about time for Him to turn back to the Jews who do, and open their eyes. He calls them 'the remnant.' He will make of them the greatest nation in the world."

"You believe that?"

"I do."

"Why don't you want your nation to be the greatest?"

Bill smiled gently in the darkness.

"It's not a question of me and my wants. This is God's plan, not something I dreamed up. There's a lot more to explain, Sam, old boy. I can't give it all tonight. If you haven't had enough we'll go on another time. But — Sam! There's not much time. Tomorrow is almost here."

CHAPTER 11

There were two letters for Verna in her mail box next morning. One bore her hometown postmark; the other was a note from Rose.

She hesitated and opened Rose's first.

"Dear Verna, Please stop at my desk after breakfast."

That could mean almost anything.

The other was from her mother.

"Dear VernaMae: Pleze rite. Dont hold it agin your father that he dint tell you already. Its hard enuf havin Rich gone. Weel see you Thanksgivin time. Yours truly mother."

Tears rose to Verna's eyes but she brushed them away and set her lips bitterly. There was just time enough to run over to see Rose before class.

"I wonder what she wants?" Verna had a vague feeling of guilt. Did Rose know that she had been out last night with Colley Corbett? Somehow she had a feeling that Rose would not approve. Colley had tried to kiss her good night but she slid out of his grasp and inside the building. Perhaps Rose had seen her.

"I know you haven't a minute," smiled Rose. "I won't keep you. I just wanted to let you know that I would love to have you come home with me for the Thanksgiving holidays, if you haven't made other plans."

"Oh!" Verna colored in delighted surprise.

She's really charming, almost beautiful, when she smiles, thought Rose. *I'd like to make her feel like smiling more often.*

"Thank you very much," replied Verna primly. Actually she was more than a little scared of accepting. "I — I'm not just sure yet. I had a letter — "

"That's perfectly all right," interrupted Rose. "Just let me know when you decide. You will be most welcome."

Verna left for her class with a warm feeling about her heart. To think that she had a real invitation from a college girl! That sort of friendliness and fun was what her English teacher had told her about. Perhaps she really would find some of it for herself at last.

In spite of the fact that exams were upon them, Verna could scarcely keep her mind on history that morning. Her mother's letter had disturbed her more than she wanted to admit to herself. She was firmly determined not to go home, or write. She blamed her mother almost as much as her father. Even though she was aware of the tyrannical hold he had over his wife, Verna was sure that if she had been in her mother's place, she would have sneaked a letter off to her daughter, husband or no husband.

The invitation from Rose sounded delightful, although she knew perfectly well that her family would be up in arms to know that she even considered visiting in *auslandish* territory — "Chews" at that — where there was also an *auslandish* young man.

That evening she confided to Edda, "Guess what! I have an invitation for the Thanksgiving holidays."

Edda whirled on her. "Where?"

"Rose asked me to go home with her."

Edda's nostril curled. "Don't start running with *her*. Besides, you're coming to New York with me for over Thanksgiving." Edda's eyes narrowed. But Verna did not notice.

"With *you!*" Verna's mouth dropped open in utter amazement.

"Yes, with me. It's time you saw something of the big town. It'll do you more good than anything else."

"Oh, I wouldn't know how to act. And I don't have the clothes!"

"Just watch me. And don't worry about clothes. I

116

have more than I know what to do with at home. My shoes fit you and there will be dresses galore.

"I — I'm pretty big for your dresses," objected Verna shyly. She mustn't hurt the hand that was helping her, but she was determined not to wear that tight red dress again. She had got one look at it when she got home. Had Sam seen her?

"They're wearing 'em tight now. But you are rather tubby. You ought to reduce."

Verna sighed. There were so many new obstacles, every hour, it seemed. Would she ever make the grade?

"Well, I thank you very much. I never dreamed of such a thing. You are very kind." Verna kept piling on the thanks, trying to elicit some cordiality from her would-be hostess. But Edda had turned to creaming her face and examining it carefully in the mirror. Verna might have been absent for all the attention she paid her.

Again Verna felt as if she had been slapped. But a holiday in New York City! That was beyond her wildest imaginings. It was not in her to refuse it. She must devise a gracious refusal for Rose Goldman.

Rose expressed genuine disappointment next morning. "But another time, perhaps?" she smiled.

Verna left her regretfully. Was she foolish to turn down such a warm invitation for one that might keep her in hot water and ill humor the whole weekend? But glamor beckoned. She had made her decision.

When Saturday night arrived, Edda produced the red jersey dress again.

"Oh, not that!" exclaimed Verna. "I mean — it's rather — uh — I guess I've put on weight since I came here. I don't want to stretch it all out of shape for you."

"So what? Put it on. Colley said he was dying to see you in it again. He really fell like a ton of bricks for you, girl. Make the most of it. If you don't learn the score with him you'll never learn it with anyone."

117

"But it's too — "

"Oh, be quiet!" commanded Edda sharply. "I'm the one that gives the orders around here. If it was too small I'd tell you. You look great in it."

Verna was hurt and uneasy.

When the fellows came for them, Edda made an excuse to take Colley aside. "Look, man," she warned him, "you don't know what you're taking on. This kid is so square you'll skin your shins on her. Go easy at first and you'll get farther with her. We'd better skip the Grotto tonight and go to the State. I don't know what's on there, but we'll have to handle her with kid gloves. I might want to use her sometime or I wouldn't care."

Colley gave an assured grin. "Trust Colley," he replied.

No one could have been more solicitous. By the time they reached the theatre Verna was almost at ease again. But she glanced at one of the ads of next week's show and gasped. Colley laughed.

"They always exaggerate the ads," he explained. "Don't worry. Besides, if we don't like the show we can leave."

That was reassuring; Verna's whole life of Thou shalt nots had risen up in judgment. She felt as if she were entering the pit itself.

The first picture was a comedy and she thoroughly enjoyed it. She didn't even realize that Colley's arm was snugly around the back of her chair. It did her good to forget everything in hearty laughter. Then came the feature.

It turned out to be a documentary of communist agents infiltrating the schools of America. Verna was fascinated and shocked to watch the indoctrination of school children. Colley kept trying to attract her attention to himself by various flattering remarks in her ear. It was annoying for she didn't want to miss the plot. Gradually she noticed that Edda, on her other side, was growing fidgety. She kept whispering to Tracy Posden. Finally she gave out that she was bored. "Let's get out of here. This picture stinks!"

"Okay with me," agreed Tracy, and Colley followed suit.

"Oh-h!" objected Verna softly. "I think it's fascinating. I'd like to see how it comes out. Say, Edda, doesn't he sound something like Mr. Karpen?"

Edda gave her a venomous glare.

"I'm getting *out!*" she declared and clambered over the rest to the annoyance of the people behind her. Tracy followed, and Verna felt that there was probably nothing she could do but follow, especially as it was Colley's car that they came in.

"Let's go out to the drive-in," Edda spoke it as a command rather than a suggestion.

Why, wondered Verna to herself, *does everyone take orders from her? Why do I do it myself? She always seems to be able to make anyone do what she wants. It must be she's a natural leader.* Verna sighed.

The picture at the drive-in was a rather vulgar triangle. The sordidness of it repelled Verna. She grew very quiet. Once she changed her position and glanced back to see how the others were liking it. She caught her breath in horrified astonishment. Edda was lolling intimately in Tracy's arms; neither was watching the picture.

Colley had chain-smoked steadily. Now he turned to her.

"Tired, baby?" He was being discreetly gentle. "Put your head down."

He drew her toward him and attempted to place her head on his shoulder.

She jerked away. "I'm not tired," she retorted. It was too dark for him to see her mouth, pursed up again in the old way. She was most unhappy.

"Oh, come on, baby, can't you be a little friendly? Don't be such a square."

There was that hated word again. Was this the sort of thing she must submit to in order not to be a square? If she cared the least bit for Colley Corbett it wouldn't be so bad. She forced herself to smile at him.

"I am friendly," she offered timidly. "You have been very nice to me."

"Then *make,* girl! I've been yearning for you all evening. Like I told you, you're a doll in that red dress." He laid his enormous arm about her shoulders again and let it lie there without pulling her closer. He was quite sure he was obeying Edda's instructions implicitly.

To Verna it was as pleasant as having a steam roller curl itself around her neck. But she said nothing more. If this was what a girl had to put up with to make friends and have dates, she could learn to stick it out as well as the next one.

"Say," he said after a few minutes, "I know what we need. I'm thirsty. How about you? Shall I go get some nice cold juice?"

"That would be wonderful! I am thirsty."

"How about you two?" He flung the question at the back seat.

"Okay," responded Edda.

Verna was relieved to have him gone. But she still felt uncomfortable with those two making love back there. She had had no idea that Edda was so fond of Tracy Posden. Perhaps she was engaged to him. That must be it. Verna tried to watch the picture but it sickened her.

Colley came back very soon. "I got straws; want one?" he offered Verna.

"Yes, I'll take one. Thank you."

Gratefully she took the cool little can and drew a long refreshing swallow. It tasted strange. It wasn't orange juice, or pineapple. In fact, it seemed more like apple juice, but it must be spoiled. She waited to hear whether any of the rest noticed it.

Colley gulped his down and opened another. Nobody mentioned that anything was the matter with the drink. She tried to read the label, but there was not enough light. She was glad of the straw. She could merely pretend to be drinking; it was most unpleasant. She hoped it wouldn't make her sick.

"Now you'll feel like snuggling a little, won't you, baby?" Colley's arm was around her again, compelling. He moved over closer to her and before she knew it his thick wet lips were on hers.

She writhed quickly away and like a flash she slapped his face. All he did was laugh. "Say, you're cute when you look like that. Come on, baby, be nice."

"You leave me alone!" Verna spat out her fury. "If you don't take me home now I'll get out and walk."

Edda's chortle issued from the back seat. "The threat of a true lady from time immemorial! Let's go, Colley. It's bedtime."

"Okay, okay," replied Colley. "I didn't do anything wrong, did I?"

"No, but if you will play with sharp edges you'll get hurt. Let's go. It's almost deadline for the dorm and I've got to get my little sister back safely."

To Verna's relief the evening was over.

She lay in bed and fumed to herself. Edda had said very little after they got back. She made light of Colley's advances and explained as if to a child that every boy expected some return for the money he spent on his girl.

"That sounds like — prostitution!" cried Verna.

Edda gave her usual moan of exasperation. Verna said no more. She lay awake for hours, alternately exultant over the fact that at last she was really living, and consumed with shame over what Sam or Rose would think if they had seen her on the date tonight. How was she to tell who was right? It was weeks since she had dared to kneel beside her bed and try to pray.

121

CHAPTER 12

Exams came and went. Verna won her A in history, then went on to pile up more A's, in English, biology, and even calculus. Each time she received her mark she would triumphantly display it to Edda. But it was most disconcerting; Edda had A's in her courses also.

There was only one test left to take, and that was political science. She was nervous over it, because she felt that Edda, being so friendly with the teacher, and having been chosen by him as "observer" in the group meeting, must in the nature of things know more than she did. Verna practically memorized the text. Then she made careful notes to study during breakfast and she pored over them even while she walked to class. But there were lists of terms new to her which simply would not stay in their places in her mind. She took one last desperate glance at the notes and tucked the little cards in her blouse pocket behind her handkerchief. The exam sheets were given out. Verna's heart sank. Long columns of true or false questions! She never felt sure of those, because it seemed to her the statements were often ambiguous. And on the second sheet were matching questions, all of them referring to the terms she had struggled so hard to get.

I'll never pass this! she thought in panic. Her mind seemed to congeal. The more she wrestled with the true and false statements the more confused she became. After less than an hour she saw Edda confidently turn in her paper and sail out of the room.

Disheartened, in a cold sweat, she took a deep breath and started at the beginning again.

I'll take them as if they were brand new and I was

122

fresh; perhaps I'll get a new perspective, she decided. She went carefully through the first page, changing only one or two of her answers.

Then she turned the page.

The same old perplexing terms stared up at her and seemed to seize her mind and twist it, wringing it dry of any thoughts at all. If only she could get a glimpse again of those little cards. Everything she needed was there, set down in order. All it would take would be a glance to get her started off right. She thought of the tone of Edda's voice when she would say, "You thought that exam was tough? It was a snap. I finished in no time."

She couldn't let that happen. She *had* to beat Edda. Tears began to well up. They filled her eyes. They mustn't drop on her exam sheet. She reached for her handkerchief. There were the little cards, so handy. She deftly blotted at her eyes and held the bit of cloth in her left hand as if to use it again. Swiftly she glanced at the neat rows of items and checked them off. How simple. Then she blotted once more at her eyes as if she had trouble clearing her vision. That gave her a chance to turn the cards.

In a very few minutes she was able to complete the test and turn in her paper. She knew that she had the right answers. After all, lots of the kids cheated.

She passed Sam on the way out and suddenly a wave of shame enveloped her. What would Sam think of what she had done? She almost ran out of the room. She was glad that she had to rush to get packed in time to make the train for New York. She didn't want to think. Never in all her life before had she cheated to get her good grades. She felt she never wanted to look Mr. Karpen in the face again. She tried to force her thoughts toward the coming holiday.

But on the train Edda met other friends and scarcely spoke to Verna the whole trip. Then less than two hours after they arrived at Edda's home, a handsome fifteenth floor apartment overlooking Central Park, her hostess sailed out on a date with an old friend leaving Verna alone with her thoughts.

A long time Verna stood at the dark window watching little bright dots go darting back and forth, back and forth, on the street far below. But for her there was no beauty in the jeweled display; all she could see was that terrible page of lying answers staring up at her. She felt she would rather have an F than have to live with it. What could she do about it? Nothing now. She had a feeling that Sam was looking at it, too, over her shoulder, and that he turned and gave her that straightforward gaze, right in her eyes, that made her feel that he looked through into her soul. She writhed. He must never know — yet she would give anything if she could go to him now and tell him all about it. Why Sam? She didn't know, except that he seemed to understand; he knew all about her and didn't reject her. Finally in desperation she went to the living room. There one whole wall was lined with books. Eagerly she began to revel in them. This was what she had always wanted. Enough books and time to read them.

She read until her eyes burned. Hearing a noise, she glanced at the clock. Eleven-thirty. The door opened and in came a tall, thin, handsome man of forty or so, expensively clad, with graying temples and gray green eyes like Edda's.

He looked mildly surprised, but spoke cordially enough.

"A friend of Edda's from college? She didn't tell me she was bringing a guest. But that's Edda." He shrugged deprecatingly, and sat down on the other end of the big luxurious couch.

Verna smiled. She didn't like to say to the girl's own father, "Yes, she isn't very thoughtful." She was not aware that her face said it.

How was she to converse with this fine-looking

124

stranger, so evidently sophisticated. From one of Mrs. Ross's little talks on orientation she remembered that a good way to get acquainted with people was to ask questions and find out the other person's interest.

"What is your business, Mr. Wittig?" she began. She sounded so like a clerk filling out a form that he gave a serio-comic smile.

"I'm a banker," he answered as if he were speaking to a child.

"Oh." Verna wondered what came next. "Uh — is your business doing well?"

"As a matter of fact, no," he replied politely, hiding his amusement.

"Oh, that's too bad," sympathized Verna. "What seems to be the matter? Is the market down?" She recalled the phrase from her high school math course.

What on earth! thought Mr. Wittig. *This girl must be an economics major.* He hedged a bit and then, upon her continued interest, began to launch into a serious discussion of business.

She gave such concentrated attention that he found himself going into detail. It was almost a relief to him to have some one who was willing to listen to his woes. As Verna asked more and more questions, intelligent and concerned, he revealed his very real terror at world conditions.

His handsome brows knitted while he chewed away at his unlighted cigar. Every few minutes he would cross the room and pour himself a drink. Verna was not as shocked as she might have been had she not already learned to know Edda. She soon began to realize that the poor man was on the verge of a nervous breakdown.

"No one knows what's going to happen next!" He fidgeted as he talked and twitched his foot up and down. "The whole world may be blown to bits before tomorrow." His voice rose tense and shrill. "There may not be anyone left at all. Well, so what?" He laughed bitterly. "But I am only scaring you, young lady. You have your life to live. Enjoy it while you can."

For the first time in weeks Verna forgot her own troubles. Years of training in her church, meager though its teaching had been, rose up to combat such a hopeless philosophy.

"Oh, Mr. Wittig," she leaned forward earnestly, "there will be judgment, but the *whole* world will not be blown up. The Bible says it won't."

He gave an amused smile. "Really?"

"No, it says that God will shorten the days of tribulation *or else* there wouldn't be anyone saved."

"Well, well. That is most interesting. But I guess no one can tell that for sure."

"Oh, it's true. It's in the Bible somewhere — I'm not sure just where," she twisted her hands in an embarrassed effort to remember enough to help him. "The important thing is that you take Christ as your Saviour before all this happens."

"My dear young lady, you are quite a preacher. You must have been listening to radio sermons." He tossed his head and arose.

(*Just exactly the way Edda does,* thought Verna.)

"Could be they have something. Who knows? Well, I guess I'll be getting off to bed. You are very welcome here. I hope you enjoy your stay."

Verna thought he staggered a little as he left the room. For some minutes her thoughts were taken up with the poor man's wretchedness. For some reason her own distress seemed to have lessened. She wondered whether she had done wrong to try to talk to him as she did. Edda would scold her if she knew.

Then as she went off to bed herself, the old depression began to seize her once more. She became engrossed in her own sorrows; and she no sooner crawled into bed than the memory of that cheated exam came to pester her. She tossed and wrestled with her conscience. She knew cheating didn't fit with what she had just been saying. What could she do about it?

In the Goldman home there was great anticipation of the Thanksgiving holidays. Harry Jr. would be there with his wife and the new grandson. Sam and Rose were driving home with Sam's roommate. The elder Goldmans had always made the children's friends more than welcome.

Mama Goldman had Rose on her mind. "I'll know as soon as I see her," she confided to her husband, "whether there's really anything wrong with Rosie. When you haven't seen a person for quite a while you can read them better."

But Mama was not prepared for the glow in Rose's eyes, nor the lilt of joy in her footsteps. She watched as Bill helped Rose out of the car and up the steps. Her heart gave a premonitory leap. Then it was love! Well, that was not as bad as some things might have been. But she took one look at the blond giant smiling down at her daughter and her knees almost gave way beneath her. Quite obviously he was *meshumed*. But that did not mean that the brave, determined woman did not observe every detail about Bill all the while she was bustling about welcoming the rest and making everyone comfortable. Sam had written a great deal about this young man, but Rose had never mentioned him. That was almost proof in itself. Was it too late? Some parents would have sent Rose to her room until the company was gone, but Mama Goldman would wait to hear the truth from her daughter's own lips.

Bill had spent hours alone on his knees, up on the big old flat rock, before he accepted this invitation. He knew well what issues were at stake, what barriers of culture and creed would stand between him and these friends he had learned to love. But he finally decided that unless he made the first move neither he nor they could make the second. So he went, with

127

peace in his heart and a brilliant smile of sincere cordiality on his face.

With a great deal of apprehension, the Goldman parents talked it over that Wednesday night and decided to wait until after the family Thanksgiving dinner to bring up the subject. They felt that it was only fair to Rose not to jump to conclusions. They would wait.

As they all gathered around on Thursday for the festive meal, there was a hushed moment before Papa took up the knife to carve. Mr. Goldman's solemn voice invoked the blessing of Jehovah on the food and on the house.

Bill's steady, joyous smile seemed like a glowing lamp that lit up that end of the table. Rose could not keep her eyes away from him. *It's as if his eyes were saying all the while "Shalom! Shalom!" Oh, how I love him. And I'm sure he loves me.* Then the terrifying thought would be sure to pop up its ugly head, *But what will Mama and Papa say?*

Sam, oblivious of his sister's involvement, talked eagerly on about college. The new baby, too, kept drawing their attention. Once Mama Goldman caught Bill's eyes on Rose while she was cuddling the baby. A cold chill went through the mother. She was quite sure now. To think this terrible thing had happened to them. They had always been one; how could Rosie, their Rosie, have let herself look with desire on one who in spite of his statuesque form, his head like a Greek god, and his eyes like heaven's blue, was a tempter in disguise. For what awful sin had this thing been visited upon the house of Goldman? Had they failed to warn their daughter?

"Now Mama," soothed her husband in the kitchen after dinner, "just wait. Wait until we can talk to Rosie herself. It is not fair to her to be so upset. It may not be true at all." But Papa had little assurance in his own mind that she was mistaken.

128

They were all gathered around the fireplace in the living room after dinner, watching the baby crawl from one to another.

What a family! thought Bill with a sigh. He thought of his own barren childhood and the wasted years of his teens. "If only . . . Oh Lord," he cried silently, "let me be able to introduce them to Jesus Christ. Open their hearts and open my lips."

Sam turned on the television. "Maybe the football game is still on," he suggested.

Penn and Cornell were in their last quarter of play, in the Philadelphia stadium, when all at once the picture blanked out.

"We interrupt this program to bring you a special bulletin. An attack has been threatened on Israel by the combined forces of Russia and Red China. The United Arab Republic is also on the verge of military action against Israel. The reserves of the United Nations Forces have been alerted and the Security Council has been called into special session."

The message was repeated while the little group sat with their mouths open in horror. Bill glanced at Sam. Mama Goldman's hands trembled as she hugged her grandson to her. "That means Yehudi will be in danger again. Ach, what will become of his boy David? And Mordecai! My poor brother!"

Tears coursed slowly down Mama Goldman's face, in spite of her struggles to hold them back. Her husband rose and went over to her and patted her shoulder. Even more than for the news of danger to Israel she was overflowing with distress for the threatened disaster to their happy family, and Papa Goldman knew it. It would ease her nerves to cry a little.

Sam looked at Bill and opened his mouth to speak. Then he closed it again. Sam had thought a great deal about what Bill had told him. Finally he had demanded to see the prophecies. He was inclined to believe that the time of their fulfillment was actually

129

imminent, as Bill had said. Would it be better to raise the question himself or let Bill do it? Sam was aware it might cause controversy.

"Bill and I have been reading the Bible," he ventured. Then without waiting for a reaction, he plunged on. "Did you know that Russia and her satellites are mentioned by the prophet Ezekiel? He said they would attack Israel after she was established as a nation again. Ever hear that, Harry?" He turned to his brother as being most likely to be liberal in his thinking. Again, without waiting for him to reply, he went on. "After all, it's no wonder that the Arabs have it in for Israel. They are descended from Esau and from Ishmael. Look how Jacob and Esau quarreled with each other; and how Ishmael made fun of Isaac."

"But it was Isaac, not Ishmael, and Jacob, not Esau, to whom God gave the land and renewed the covenant!" put in Bill. There was a glad ring of confidence in his tone.

Mama Goldman pricked up her ears. Could it be that her Sam had even maybe proselytized this handsome young man? How proud she would be of Sam. And that would solve her worries over Rosie.

Rose listened in wonder. The boys sounded just like Mrs. Ross. Had Sam, too, begun to stride across traditional lines? Instinctively she began to share her mother's fear lest one of their number disgrace the family. How strange, when she herself had been more than half inclined to turn to the Christian faith. Could it be that the very dread itself was only a tradition? Actually, she would be glad if she found she could talk these things over with her brother and not have to hide in her own heart any longer what would seem to her family a shame.

Suddenly Harry spoke up. His voice held disillusionment and a tinge of bitterness. "I'm not so sure any more that the covenant ever meant anything. Certainly the services in the synagogue do not tend to draw our

130

young people any nearer to God. Perhaps not all synagogues are the same, and I'll admit I haven't been going much lately since I've been so busy, but when I was younger and used to go, I never felt as if I had been near to God. The Rabbis read the Law in such a monotonous voice none of us ever listened, even the grownups. The women up in the gallery yakked so loud you couldn't hear if you wanted to."

"Yes," put in Rose. "You hear more gossip up there among the women than you do over the clothes line. And the girls do nothing but talk about the boys."

Mama and Papa looked sad and shocked.

"And when they choose a cantor it's like a circus midway," went on Harry, warming up when he found he had support. "As I look back on it now, it seems irreverent. In my opinion the cantor should be one who lives close to God, not the one with the loudest voice. Why, Mama, I don't know one time when I ever chose to do right because of a Temple service. The only reason I have been decent is because you and Papa taught us to do right."

"My children!" cried Mama Goldman, frightened in earnest now. "I have never heard you talk like this. Are you then ashamed of the faith of your fathers?"

"No, Mama," replied Sam with quiet respect, "but the way it is carried on now, I don't believe *is* the real faith of our fathers. It is degenerated into a sort of empty form. There is no life there."

Seeing an opportunity during this family forum to try out the new ideas she had gained, Rose innocently flung another bomb.

"After all, we have to admit that we have no blood sacrifices any more. We can't, of course, until — " She caught herself for she was mentioning aloud the goal that had long been a secret in many Jewish families. Then she continued boldly — "until the Temple is rebuilt. And God said that the life is in the blood, that it was the blood that made atonement for sin. All these hundreds of years we've had no blood sacrifices. All right, then! We've had no real atonement. Yom Kippur is a farce."

The others, including Bill, looked at Rose in amazement.

But Papa Goldman knew what his wife was thinking. "My children!" he rebuked them. "This is a disgrace that I never thought would come to my house. You have dishonored the Law and the Prophets. Until you can come back to your senses we will not discuss this further."

"But Papa!" objected Harry Jr. "It's not the Truth we are criticizing, only the careless way people treat the Truth."

"None of you ever questioned until you went off to college," stated Mama in a flat tone from which all joy had been drained. "It must be from going with *meshumed* people." She glared straight at Bill. Then she gathered her sleeping grandson up in her arms and in stately sorrow she left the room.

There was a strained silence. Sam got up and turned off the TV which he had lowered while they talked.

"Let's go out and take a walk, Bill," he suggested. "You coming, too, Rose?"

Rose caught up her jacket and joined them. Harry's wife went to take a nap. Papa and his eldest son were left to stare at the fire.

CHAPTER 13

Friday morning in New York was rainy and raw. Edda wasn't up yet. Verna stood and watched the drops drizzle down the pane. What a dreary place this was; what a really unhappy life Edda must have lived. No mother, no brothers and sisters, no real home. Her father was pleasant enough, but Edda had told her that he wasn't often there.

Verna began to wish she had gone with Rose instead of coming to New York. She had expected a nice Thanksgiving dinner yesterday and maybe a party. But apparently Thanksgiving day to the Wittigs was just another day. When her hostess finally did arise she made coffee and scrambled eggs; not even toast, because she said she was dieting.

"You can get whatever you see in the refrigerator," she said carelessly.

Verna almost wept. At home there was always plenty of good food, and on Thanksgiving day a turkey or at least a big chicken dinner, when all the family put aside small irritations and gathered around. Her father asked a blessing, gruffly, to be sure, but there was a spirit of oneness and gratitude. Verna had to struggle with something in her throat as she realized that those days were gone forever. She could never feel the same toward her family. If she did go back, Richard would not be there. She hurried to the kitchen to hide her face from Edda.

As she munched a piece of toast and jam — alone, for Edda ate quickly and went out — she wondered what it would have been like at Rose's home. Perhaps Rose would ask her another time. If she did, she would go, in spite of the nasty remarks Edda would make. If anything, Verna had more of a comradely feeling for the Jewish young people because of being outside the camp herself.

She was quite taken aback when Edda gave her to understand that when she was home she always slept till noon, went shopping for clothes every afternoon and out on a date every night. Verna began to wonder why she had been invited.

"When can I go sight-seeing?" she ventured wistfully during the few minutes' conversation she had with her hostess between flittings.

133

"Suit yourself," shrugged Edda. Could it be that the motherless girl did not realize how a guest should be treated? Verna compared her lack of cordiality to the stiff, yet hospitable welcome guests had always received in her own home.

"How would I get to the Statue of Liberty?" she asked hesitantly.

"Take a taxi, of course. Though why you want to view that hunk of granite is more than I know," scoffed Edda. "Or take a Fifth Avenue bus. Ride to the end of the line and back like a hick, if you like. You'll see most of the city that way."

The city fascinated Verna but it was terrifying to think of venturing out alone into the maelstrom of buses, taxis, El trains and roaring trucks, to say nothing of the masses and masses of people. But after two days of doing nothing but reading and walking in the park, Saturday afternoon she finally screwed up her courage to try it. She came home exhausted from the noise and from nervousness over wondering whether she could find her way home again.

Forlornly she fixed herself a tuna fish and tomato salad for supper. Then she hunted up her book again and read until her eyes were tired. She was beginning to work up a good case of self-pity when she suddenly heard the key in the lock.

Edda home at nine-thirty? She generally stayed out until two or even three on her dates.

"Well, guess who I met!" cried Edda as if she had never been less than cordial. "Colley Corbett and his brother Lee. Is *he* ever the cool cat! Come on, we're going out. Lee knows a lot of people here and there and we'll do the town. I guess you haven't had much to do, have you?"

Such unprecedented thought for her comfort melted Verna. The idea of seeing someone she knew, even if it was only Colley Corbett, was delightful.

"We've got to find you some clothes, but first I've got

to have a drink. I'm bushed." Edda went to the polished mahogany cupboard and took out a bottle and two glasses. "Have some?" she offered.

Verna was startled. In spite of having cast away the cords of parental training to some extent, there were still some standards that she clung to. According to her traditions, liquor in any form had belonged to only the very wicked of the world. Now what was she going to do?

Stalling for time, she answered in a small voice, "No, thank you."

Suddenly Edda set her glass down. "Look here," she said in her most commanding manner, "you're not going square again on me! If we go out tonight, you're going to go along and do as the Romans or else you don't go. I brought you up here so you could learn a few things and I intend to see that you do. I've been off here and there; but now there's a chance to get out, let's have no squeamishness. Now," she came over and sat down patiently beside Verna, a small glass in her hand, "I'm going to explain to you. This is only sherry. It can't possibly do you any harm to sip a little. It isn't like strong liquor. You don't have to take a lot, you know, just sip it now and then so as not to look square. Don't you see?"

Verna half nodded, helplessly. What was it this girl did to her to make things look so different?

"And besides," Edda flung a pious note into her tone, "I've heard that the Bible itself says that it's all right to drink on certain occasions. Now come, it will be like a tonic for you. I can see you're depressed. I shouldn't have left you alone so much in a strange town." Edda actually apologizing? And quoting the Bible? Or trying to, at least. It was unprecedented.

Slowly, with many a misgiving, Verna took the glass. "That's it, just a little. It is good, isn't it?"

Verna unwillingly admitted that it was. She took

135

another sip. Edda went on chattering, describing where they would go. "We'll do a whole list of night clubs."

"Won't that be very expensive?" asked Verna. "I remember your telling Colley he couldn't afford many drinks last week."

"Oh Schiffelgruber! F'reaven's sakes. I didn't mean *money*. Corbetts are loaded. I meant he — he oughtn't to drink *much*."

"Oh!" replied Verna, relieved.

"They'll be by about ten-thirty for us."

"Ten-thirty!" repeated Verna in astonishment.

"Yes," laughed her hostess. "You'll find that nothing even starts in New York until nearly midnight. That's why everyone sleeps till noon."

Verna shook her head incredulously. But even the few swallows of the sherry, unaccustomed as she was to it, had already taken away her depression and things seemed considerably more cheerful. Edda really was kind-hearted underneath. She was just thoughtless. "Maybe *I* could help *her!*" Verna was quite pleased with the idea.

There was no red jersey to struggle into this time. The dress Edda produced was brilliant green, a strapless affair, with a gorgeous full, floating skirt. Gold slippers with heels completed the outfit.

Verna gasped. Excited to the point of speechlessness, she held it up to her.

"It does look pretty with my hair, doesn't it?"

"Marvelous," agreed Edda, already busy with her own garments.

Verna posed a little, holding it this way and that. "But I wonder if I can get unto it."

"It's almost too big for me," said Edda. "That's why I rarely wear it. I'm sure you can make it. You have to expect to be a little uncomfortable, you know, when you're really dressed."

Verna hastened off to prepare.

When she was finally arrayed, her plumpness bulging

136

upward more than a little above the upper line of the dress, Edda herself exclaimed over how stunning she looked. "And here — these belong with it." She brought out a set of huge earrings and a necklace of green stones set in gold.

"Wait till your boy friend sees you now!"

Edda was delighted with her own success in having chosen the right combination for her protegé. Edda herself was in pale flesh color.

Verna's breath came fast. At last she was really at the top! They both looked just like the pictures in magazines that she had pored over since coming to school. Before that she had rarely had a glimpse of magazines. Her father would not permit them in the house.

She was relieved to find that the wine had not made her raving drunk. Actually, she felt no different at all.

But Colley Corbett noticed her high spirits and bright eyes when he stepped into the apartment. His brother was waiting below with the car.

He whistled when he saw Verna. Then he simply stood still and admired her with his eyes. Verna colored and giggled. She grabbed a light wrap that Edda had laid out for her. Colley seized it and folded it close around her shoulders, caressingly. He did not seem as rough and crude as he had back at college. Was it because he wore a tuxedo? Or because she had got used to life as other people lived it, in these two short days in New York? Verna looked forward to an ecstatic evening.

Oliver Snead's roommates would have been astonished if they could have had a glimpse that evening into the living room of Dean Wittig. A small-featured mouse of a young fellow sat almost lost in one of the dean's big overstuffed foam rubber chairs. His funny beady little eyes behind his round-eyed spectacles gazed at the dean with a troubled stare while he listened to his uncle, the great multi-millionaire Ebenezer Snead, of Bulldog Equipment fame, storm at the college official. His uncle looked like a big white-haired Oliver, charged with a massive voltage of power.

"Oliver," commanded his uncle in a voice that billowed, "I want you to tell Dean Wittig yourself exactly what you told me."

Oliver twisted in his downy seat and edged to the front of it to get a better take-off for his speech.

"Well, thir, I'll try. I'm thtupid, of course, and I'm not thure of all that wath implied, but I do have a pretty good memory, thir, and I can give it to you almoth word for word."

The dean suppressed a sensation of repugnance. It would never do to antagonize the Snead millions for they carried votes on the college board. But he simply could not stand the sight of this puny youth. He listened with seeming concern as Oliver repeated the gist of Edward Karpen's talks, both in class and at his special "club" meetings. Wittig was bored, since the elder Snead had already given him an identical recitation of what the old man called "this subversive anti-Americanism." Wittig's lip curled.

With his brow drawn down and his pencil doodling subconsciously, Dean Wittig considered the matter and promised the tycoon in conciliatory fashion that the professor in question would surely be brought on the carpet and thoroughly checked.

"Fine, fine. That's all I wanted. As long as the authorities are informed, that should take care of the matter. Now," Mr. Snead arose and turned toward the door; Oliver, on the other side of Mr. Wittig's desk, followed suit, "I must apologize for taking your time on a holiday. Thank you. Good evening."

Outside the door and beyond the grounds, riding in luxurious ease, Oliver ventured a question.

"Uncle," he asked speculatively, "why do you thuppoth Dean Wittig was drawing hammerths and thickles on hith dethk blotter?"

Ebenezer Snead looked down at his nephew with pride. "Oliver," he stated with confidence, "you are going to make a smart man. A very smart man. The answer to your question is for you to find out."

But if any of the students had been asked whether Oliver Snead was at the club meetings, or even a member of the class, they couldn't have told, for the life of them.

Later that same evening, Dean Wittig put in a long distance call to New York, person to person, for Edward Karpinsky. It was a long time before he could be located. He was seated at a table in an off-beat night club when the waiter brought him the phone.

"Call for you, Mr. Karpinsky, sir." With careful respect the waiter placed the instrument on the table.

"Ed," Dean Wittig spoke in a muffled voice, "you'll have to pipe down. There's been a bit of a stink here in the wrong quarters. Take it easy. Nothing serious. Just thought I'd let you know before you come back."

"Okay. That'll be fine." Mr. Karpen smiled gaily at his table full of guests. "I'll have it looked after by Monday. Thank you." He handed the waiter a handsome tip and went on with his conversation. But when two young couples entered the room later on, he eyed all four carefully before he went over to their table and drew up a chair.

Verna thought him very handsome in his immaculate dinner suit. She was still awed by seeing men in sophisticated attire chatting gallantly to the ladies in their company. A vision of her own father and brothers flitted across the back of her mind. Imagine her father in clothes like these drawing out a chair for her mother, making flattering little compliments close to her ear as he seated her, or sometimes stealing a little kiss on the back of her neck, as Verna had seen one middle-aged man do at a table over in the corner. His wife blushed and smiled; at least she assumed it was his wife. She could not picture her oldest brother, for instance, gracefully handing Tillie Getz into his old jalopy, chivalrously holding her skirt away from the door as he closed it. Verna noted all the little niceties of the new life she was tasting and wondered: were they real or were they superficial? She decided that in any case, they were much to be desired.

It occurred to her once to wonder how Sam would appear in a place like this. It was hard to imagine him here. He was quite unlike her brothers; he was most courteous, but she had a feeling he would not choose this sort of life. Why not?

Mr. Karpen let his eyes rest often on Verna. He did not identify her at first with the gauche zealot in his class. She had a figure that many girls would gladly have taken in exchange for their own carefully dieted forms, and her atmosphere of naiveté was outstanding in the midst of so many sophisticates.

When Verna realized that he was directing his attention to her she grew more excited and she laughed a little louder. She had allowed herself one very small drink in each restaurant; this was the fourth they had visited. At times Mr. Karpen seemed a bit blurry; she must be getting sleepy.

A beautiful blonde in a diaphonous gown appeared and crooned in a low whispery voice something about "Why I never saw you before" with accompanying gestures. Mr. Karpen directed a meaningful smile at Verna, straight into her eyes. Colley had left the table to speak to someone else and the professor moved over closer to her and laid his hand on hers and gently squeezed it. It seemed as if he wasn't paying any attention to the singer; he just wanted to look at her. It went to Verna's head and she smiled back, blushing ingenuously. She had never welcomed Colley's advances, but this was different; it was wonderful to be sought out by her teacher. It must be that she was really beautiful and she had never found it out before. A new thrill shot through her when he squeezed her

140

hand again as he rose to let Colley take his seat. What a wonderful evening this had turned out to be; it was more glamorous than all her dreams. She must let Edda know how very grateful she was; all her life she would remember the one who had made this possible for her. She scarcely knew that she was tired, although it was now two o'clock.

One more stop, for Edda insisted. It was strange how Edda seemed to know someone in each place they went; someone at another table to whom she "just must say hello." Of course, Edda lived here; she must have hundreds of friends. Verna's eyesight was not at its best any more; she did not observe very closely the type of persons to whom Edda spoke. But it didn't matter; everything was fabulous.

It was after three. They were finally headed back to the Wittig apartment. Verna didn't turn to look at the silent pair in the back seat. She was almost afraid to. Anyway, she was too weary, to content to let Colley's arm hold her close as he drove, crazily enough, with the other. The moon was bright; they were on the Palisades and they could just glimpse the river, a polished black band, far below. Verna thought she had never been so happy. Colley whispered something in her ear that she didn't catch.

"Colley!" she exclaimed under her breath. "Why do you look at me like that?" His hand was moving over her shoulder. "Wh — what are you *doing?*"

Suddenly she screamed and struck at him. The car careened to one side of the street, then back into the left lane. A car was coming straight at them around the curve. Edda shrieked. An arm shot past Colley's ear from the back seat and yanked the wheel just in time to veer out of the path of the other car, but the force of the turn threw the wheels off balance; the car scraped horridly along the stone wall on the right and stalled at right angles to the street. It all happened in an instant. Cars behind them squealed their tires;

a little sport car coming from the opposite direction almost climbed up on them.

"Start it quick, Coll," ordered Lee under his breath. "Let's get out of here before the cops come. Will she go?"

Miraculously the big motor responded; Colley backed and drove off, but Lee had to hold the door shut on his side.

Nobody spoke for a block or so. They were all gasping and looking behind for police.

Then Lee swore loudly and yelled at his brother, "Okay, now tell us what happened. I s'pose you know you'll pay for this, if the insurance won't hold."

"Okay, okay, I will," retorted Colley. "But they'll pay. It wasn't my fault. This she-devil here nearly blinded me."

Verna, thoroughly sobered, was trembling at the far edge of the front seat. She was a confusion of shame, terror and anger. She wouldn't even look at her escort or speak. She stared straight ahead into the darkness.

Edda, keen to scent the situation, decided to scold Colley first. She would attend to Verna later.

"I thought I warned you before, Colley Corbett!" she berated him. "You haven't the sense of an alley cat."

"Oh, shut your face!" Colley was angry all through.

They drew up at the apartment house. "Get out, you wildcat!" he hissed. He made no move to open the bent-up door for Verna. Even Lee could not budge it. She finally had to climb awkwardly over the back of the seat and slide out the back door, for Colley would not move.

Verna was angry and Edda was furious.

"What a way to end a pleasant evening!" she flung at her guest while they waited for the elevator. The lovely green gown was torn and streaked with blood from a cut on Verna's face. "Wait till I get you alone! I could claw you to bits!"

CHAPTER 14

The morning after Thanksgiving Bill waited in vain for Rose to appear. He did not feel free to ask where she was.

Sam suggested bowling and the two spent most of the afternoon at the alleys. Bill asked once, "Doesn't your sister care for bowling?"

Sam only shrugged. "I don't know that she has ever tried it." Bill did not pursue the subject further, but he had a feeling that Rose was in trouble.

As a matter of fact, Rose was shut into her mother's room all morning; she was being catechized. The door was not locked; she could have walked out at any time, but that would have broken the tradition her mother had established.

Mama Goldman wept by spells, scolded by spells, and the rest of the time she pleaded.

"But Rosie, my baby girl, Papa will find you a nice Jewish boy who would love you. He would be rich; he would give you everything a girl could wish."

"Except Bill," replied Rose patiently.

"But Rosie, you will spoil your life. It will never work, your joining with a Christian. It is forbidden. That is one reason why we Jews have had such troubles, because so many times our children have married outside. You can bring only trouble to us all, Rosie. I beg you, give him up, this Christian.

"Mama, how can I give him up when I love him? Besides, there is nothing to give up. He has never said that he loves me. He has never talked love to me at all. There is nothing to give up."

"But he will. I can see it in his eyes."

Rose brightened. A little secret smile stole through

143

the dark fog caused by her mother's harangue. But she did not answer. By now she was saying as little as possible. There was nothing more to say.

"Rosie," her mother coaxed, coming over to her and trying to draw the girl into her embrace, "do you love me and Papa?"

"Of course."

"Then promise me you will never date this man again."

"He may never ask me, Mama."

"If he does, promise me."

"I can't promise that."

"But how can you go on being a Jew at all and walk so close with a Christian?"

"I don't think I am a Jew in the way you mean, Mama."

Mama threw her apron over her head and moaned.

"Ach, it is worse than I thought! Call Papa."

"No, now listen, Mama. I love our people, you know that. I'm proud to be a daughter of Abraham; I always shall be. But I believe our people have made a terrible mistake. And I think we are suffering the consequences of it. I have read this in the Law, Mama. You can read it for yourself. Moses foretold all our sufferings."

"Rosie!" scoffed her mother. "You should know better. These Christians do not understand. They have been using our Law to teach you wrong things. The judgment Moses prophesied was carried out long ago, when we lost our kingdom."

"Yes, but God led some back to the land, and they sinned again, Mama. I can show you. It is all there. Mama, I am convinced that our Messiah is Jesus. We have rejected Him; that is why we suffer so." Rose took a deep breath. She had never expressed the thought even in her own heart before. But now she knew that it was so. She went on triumphantly to the accompaniment of her mother's low sobbing.

144

"I have read all about Him, Mama. Our rabbis are wonderful men but they have done wrong in keeping us from reading the New Testament. If you read it, you, too, will see the truth, Mama."

Suddenly her mother burst out, "It is this that Papa and I have feared. We have seen it coming. You have never been the same since you went to college. You have talked and talked about your fine Mrs. Ross. It is she who has done this wicked thing. She is an evil, cursed woman. Oh-h! My baby girl."

Just at that point Papa Goldman walked in. He read the score and his face was stern.

"Rosie, you are breaking Mama's heart. As your father, I command you never to come home again unless you are ready to give up this Christian man and all his thinking."

Rose turned white. This was the dreaded calamity that always hung over a Jewish home when one of its members dared to break tradition.

"You may stay through this holiday, but I warn you."

Mama's voice burst out in wailing. "Oh, Rosie, my baby girl, my baby girl!"

The hours of brainwashing had made Rose so uncertain in her own mind of just where she stood that the emotional outbreak only caused more confusion. She wanted to argue, to strike back. Yet she loved them.

"Mama, Papa, listen to me. I am not the only one of us who feels that way. Sam is beginning to see it, too, and you heard what Harry said yesterday. *I* am warning you. If the Christians' Jesus *is* our Messiah, it is you who must ask His forgiveness. When He comes back there will be a great mourning in Israel, and you will have to answer to Him for your part."

Rose left the room. She was stunned at her own temerity. She seized her coat and went out of the house; she must walk until she could think clearly. So many hours shut up to one person's view, to one loved voice defying her, had made her head whirl.

145

As always when she needed to be alone, she took her way out of town to a spot at the brow of a hill. She crossed a field and climbed to the top of an old three-rail wooden fence and gazed off over the valley. It reminded her of the rock behind the dorm. A rush of longing swept over her when she remembered the evening there a few short weeks before. How she wished that she could turn and see Bill coming toward her now. He was like a fortress. But she must work this thing out alone. The statement she had made to her mother just now involved no one in the whole universe but God and herself. That much she was sure of. The inherited centuries of worship, empty and traditional though they might have been sometimes, had built a strong certainty in her of the personal existence of the one true God. She had never doubted, as did some of her peers, the fulfillment of His promises, slow though they seemed in coming to pass. Now that she was faced with the possibility that the greatest of them had come to pass and her people, two millenniums ago, had missed the point, the ghastly results of that mistake were almost too appalling for her to measure.

How small she seemed. For the first time in her life she became terribly aware of her own unlikeness to the God she worshiped. What was He like, anyway? The Christians said that Jesus was His Son. "He that hath seen me hath seen the Father." That sentence had remained at the back of her mind for weeks. Mrs. Ross had quoted it. Rose had been reading the gospel of Matthew, over and over. She had to admit that there was no fault to be found in Him. Time and again the record made plain that the things He did took place "that it might be fulfilled which was written by the prophet." She knew now that whatever tomorrow might bring, for her there was no turning back.

Dusk began to settle down over the valley. She felt isolated from the whole world of human beings.

She looked up to the darkening sky. Astronauts were beginning to fly about up there. They would be alone, too. That was the thing they had always been aware of having to combat, that aloneness. And now she was going to be thrust out, from her home and family. Alone. Oh, God! Why hast Thou forsaken me? The burden of the words was like a familiar cry. She knew that they were spoken by Jesus on the cross. She had read them many times in the Psalms and in Matthew, and they had broken her heart. He knew, then, this alone feeling. But He was dead. Or was He? The record told of resurrection. Of course up to now she had only toyed with the idea of actually believing the record. But if He were the Son of God He would *have* to have eternal life in Himself. "Oh, Jesus! I do believe You are alive, somewhere. I need You. Come to my heart and let me know that I am not alone."

Into the hush of her heart came peace. A single bright star shone out with sudden glory, all quietly, like a still small voice to her soul. Rose took a deep, deep breath. She knew the Truth at last, and the Truth had made her free.

Awhile longer she sat and drank in the tranquility. Now, no matter what took place, the issues were no longer her responsibility. They were all in the hands of the One whom she could trust. *How* she knew that, she could not explain. But she knew.

She walked slowly back across the field and down the familiar streets. The gathering darkness seemed bright with glory. She glanced up at the evening star.

"You put it there!" she breathed. "You made it and You put it there for me, *Lord* Jesus."

A tender smile hovered over her lips as she opened the front door of her home.

The family was just sitting down to supper; the place at the foot of the table opposite Papa was empty. "Mama is — sick?" asked Rose with a troubled glance at her father.

"A headache," he answered gloomily.

"Where on earth have you been, Rosie?" cried Sam without too much concern. "Bill and I were about to get the sheriff with a posse to look for you." He accepted her presence with a nonchalant, welcoming glance, but Papa Goldman looked sad and stern. Harry was trying to remain completely neutral; his wife's nose was high in the air, disapprovingly.

Only Bill met Rose's eyes; instantly he guessed the truth. A silent current of understanding flowed between them; Rose saw a sudden radiance blaze up in his face. Just a flash it was and then he hid it, but she knew and he knew and that was all that mattered.

"I took a long walk," explained Rose quietly.

Later, she caught his look again and answered it.

"*Shalom* tonight?" he whispered.

She nodded, smiling back in surprise at his use of the treasured Hebrew word. "Yes, *shalom*. Perfect peace, though I don't know what tomorrow holds." He held her close an instant.

CHAPTER 15

Edda could scarcely wait until she reached her own apartment to begin her castigations. Verna had heard little swearing in her life; she was battered and stunned by the flow of curses that issued with ease from Edda's practiced lips.

"You and your fancy religious ideas!" she scoffed. "It doesn't occur to you, I suppose that the really religious angle would be to consider someone else besides your own holy self? How about my interests? What do you think I got you up here for, to antagonize all my friends? How am I going to go back to college and face Colley Corbett? And how are *you* going to face him after what you did?"

"What *I* did?" gasped Verna. "It's what he did. He was—vile!"

"Oh, fer cryin' out loud!" spouted Edda, adding an epithet or two for emphasis. "A boy doesn't want to take you out and spend money on you just to look at you. What do you think a date is for?"

"I—I didn't think it would be—horrible!" wept Verna, shuddering at the memory of Colley's unsanctioned touch.

Edda swam out of her finery with a bitter jeering hoot.

"Well, put this in your pipe and smoke it, Schiffelgruber, once for all. Underneath all the pleasant talk a man hands you, sex is all he's thinking of."

Verna caught her breath in horror. "Not *all* men, surely!"

"Well, all *I* ever met. It's a good thing you came to New York and learned a few things. How would you ever expect to get on in the world, as innocent as you were? But you'll learn. You're smart, that's for sure. And when you wake up you'll really snare 'em and enjoy it. Now get outa here or go to bed. I'm tired."

Dizzy with shock and weariness, her guest went out and closed the door. She sank on the living room couch, her eyes wild and staring. Was this, then, the realization of all her dreams? She thought last week that the whole structure of her former life had crumbled when she discovered her parent's deception for the sake of five dollars. Now the very foundations of everything she had ever considered good and right were shaken. Was it true that her own father and brothers were such as Edda had described? Could that be why her father showed so little real consideration and affection for her mother? And that nice, intellectual Mr. Karpen— surely he—and then she remembered his caress on her

149

arm. Was he actually like Colley, only maybe smarter?

She thought of the other professors at school. Suddenly they all took on a hideous writhing aspect. She shivered again. She felt as if she were wading through a sewer. She never wanted to look any of them in the face again.

Why hadn't she just stayed at home? Verna Mae wondered. If she had only known that college was going to be such a disillusioning experience! It had been so from the very first day, on the train. That seemed a long, long time ago.

All at once she saw herself as she had been that day; her antiquated hair style, an old fashioned barrette at the back of her neck; her lubberly shoes; her unpolished nails; her unbecoming garment. She had learned to revolt against all of that gracelessness. She had acquired some little skill at grooming and arranging her hair; she had worked hours at typing for other students to earn a little to buy one or two attractive dresses. She even knew how to hold her own in a conversation with other young people without dissolving in embarrassment. Was it all worth it? She was glad she had learned these things. Yet what sort of world was it into which she had emerged? Now that she had worn off some of the square corners that Sam had spoken of that first day . . . Sam! Was Sam like these others? If he were, there was no hope of ever finding a clean spot to rest, as it were, anywhere in this world.

She had tried to visualize him as he had seemed to her that first day and the afternoon up on the rock. Never once had he looked at her with eyes of greed the way Colley did, the way she had seen some of Edda's boy friends look at her, that weak-chinned Tracy Posden, for instance. Verna had innocently asked Edda after that first date whether she was engaged to him. She could still hear the ridicule in Edda's mocking laugh.

"Engaged! To that fruitcake? Deliver me."

"But I saw—uh—you were—kissing him—"

"How old are you, anyway? Wake up and listen to the birds sing!"

There was only one answer to the problem for Verna: there was nothing in her that Sam found attractive. His thought for her only sprang from his own kind heart. He had said words which she would never forget, for they were like balm to her then: "You could be a living doll, you know!" But now she saw that it was because she was *not* a living doll that he said it. He had pitied her. She did not want pity.

Weary as she was, Verna was not inclined to sleep. She was facing a crisis; her own personality was at stake, at least that was the way she knew Edda would put it. Either she was to become somebody, or sink into oblivion. Stronger than ever the memory of her grandmother's words rose to her mind. But again she pushed it under the surface. Grandmother was too old; she didn't know. The only thing to do was accept the world as it was and *make* something of herself. She would have to go all out, but she would achieve it. Her Dutch perseverance would carry her to success. She would show the whole world, Edda and her family and Sam included. But her heart was still heavy, her mind confused, and her whole being exhausted from the battle. She was aware that there would be more and more battles every day that would require every bit of grit that she had. She finally slid into bed beside Edda.

But in spite of her short night, Verna awoke early Sunday morning. She had made up her mind that she needed to have some time to herself, to think, so she dressed quickly, packed her bag, and after a snack of breakfast, she left a polite little note and took her way to the railroad station and college.

Rose did not accomplish her departure so easily. Saturday morning, when Bill gradually realized that he was *persona non grata* at the Goldman home, he con-

151

fided to Sam that he felt he should get back to work on a research assignment before Monday. Rose heard and longed to go with him, but she knew that that would only cause her parents still more grief. Sam was distressed. He was so engrossed in his own companionship with Bill that he still was unaware of any special attachment between Bill and his sister.

The news broadcast had reminded all of them of their responsibility toward Israel.

When Rose went out awhile and came back shorn, her parents took heart. Perhaps Rosie was not so *meshumed*-crazy as they had feared. Sam gave her an approving grin; Bill looked his astonishment at first glance, then his eyes showered her with admiration. Her short black hair, like sparkling jet, clung in soft waves around her head and made her look like a shaggy little boy. She had always worn a sweet dignity beyond her years. Now she seemed more approachable, younger, even piquant. Bill kept hovering about her.

It was finally decided, after strained discussion, that the three young people would start back to school early Sunday morning.

Papa Goldman called Rose into her mother's room Saturday evening before dinner. Her mother's eyes were swollen; she had not appeared among them since the morning before.

"Rosie," her father began sorrowfully, "Mama and I have talked it over; all night we have talked. We have decided to give you time. You are young and maybe this is infatuation. Puppy love you will get over. We will wait. We will not ask you to promise anything. But we know our Rosie; you will be cautious; you will do nothing foolish. Remember, oh Rosie! remember we are a people set apart by God. Remember, our people in Israel now. I have been reading about what they are suffering; you have seen trouble yourself. We need each other, Rosie!" The man was not old in years, but he looked gray and haggard and his voice shook with emotion. Tears rolled slowly down his face as he took his daughter in his arms. Would it be for the last time?

Rose kissed him and held him close.

"Father, you know I love you and Mama. This home is dearer to me than I can tell. I will promise you this —I will do nothing foolish!"

He patted her shorn head and tried to smile.

"Come here, Rosie." Her mother lay prostrated with grief where she had flung herself on the bed the day before. "I don't want my baby girl's holiday all spoiled. I do trust you, darling. I am coming down to dinner and we'll say no more about it now."

Rose hugged her and wept a little with her. But there was no feeling that all was right now between them such as there used to be when she was a little girl and confessed to a misdeed. Rose knew that there was no return for her. The only hope was that her parents would have their eyes opened, too.

An infant dawn was beginning to curl soft pink fingers exploringly about the hills when they set out on Sunday morning. Sam, for the first time, glimpsed a radiant look between the lovers and raised his brows. "So that's the way it is! Well, more power to you," he muttered under his breath. "I thought there must be more to Mom's illness than an ordinary headache."

He was silent and thoughtful and very observant for a long time. All three were hushed, sharing the world's awe at heaven's display. Once Bill let his hand fall gently over Rose's where it lay beside her on the seat. He thrilled at her answering touch. He longed to glance down to see the color rise to her cheeks. What a girl! His heart was praising the God of wonders.

He had had no opportunity yet to have a talk alone with Rose, but he knew that the peace in her face could come from one thing only and that was the Spirit of the living God of peace. The road ahead seemed paved with glory.

Sam was doing his own thinking. For the first time in his life, he felt left out among his own. Not that he wasn't glad that these two people he loved had found each other, but it was a new thing to have his sister whom he had always loved and admired, and who had always looked up to him, now choosing first to look up to another. It was not altogether a pleasant sensation. He was deeply troubled, too, over the family situation which he knew now must exist.

They stopped at a roadside coffee shop later on for a second breakfast. Rose wore her new love graciously; it seemed as if the very air at their table was charged with radiance.

At last, after Sam had addressed his friend three times and received no answer because he was gazing at Rose, Sam gave up pretending.

"Okay, you two, let's have it. I might as well be in Kalamazoo. How would you like me to take the car and go on? You might like to walk the rest of the way." He grinned and Bill looked up sheepishly.

Rose smiled ecstatically and said nothing.

"Well, it has been pretty nice here," smiled Bill, "but maybe we had better move on." He picked up the checks and helped Rose on with her coat. A fleeting wonder occurred to Rose. Did Bill always leave a ten dollar tip? Not that she cared whether he was rich or poor; she was only curious. But he slipped a mere half dollar beside his plate and followed her out. Why had he been so extravagant that day at the inn?

About the middle of the morning Bill asked, "How would you feel about stopping to worship somewhere? After all, it is Sunday morning."

"Okay with me," Sam agreed without interest.

But Rose looked radiant. "I'd love to," she said softly.

They drove slowly through two or three country hamlets. Bill seemed to be scanning the notices outside each church they passed. At length he almost stopped

154

in front of a little white frame building. He read the bulletin board and turned in at the driveway. "How about this?" he said hopefully.

Rose put her hands up and straightened her beret. "Will I do this way?" She asked the question of Bill, not Sam.

"I'll say you will!" His eyes shone.

Sam reluctantly climbed out. It seemed as if these two were rather going out of their way to overdo religion. Maybe that was what love did to you at first. He hoped they would soon recover.

At the door a rugged looking farmerish man greeted them cordially with a big calloused hand. Another showed them to seats. Sam looked around. Certainly Bill had not picked a very artistic place to worship. The windows were imitation stained glass, of lurid colors. The pews were plain pine, set on a clean painted wooden floor. A little organ that seemed almost too exhausted to breathe was being operated by a young girl too plump for her clothes.

Sam couldn't see anyone on the platform. He was curious; this was the first time he had attended a Christian service. Surely all churches were not as crude; this was a straggly little country town. The people who came in and took their places were just what one would expect in farming country, pleasant faced, friendly, sincere-looking. But there was something else besides mere friendliness, Sam decided. Was it peace? Perhaps. It must be because they were far from the madding crowds of the cities.

The room was almost full when a sturdy young man about Sam's height and build arose from where he must have been sitting behind the pulpit. He announced a hymn. The organist forced out a few bars and then they all began to sing. "What can wash away my sin? Nothing but the blood of Jesus."

How they sang! With vigor rather than harmony.

It was their bright eagerness that was thrilling. Everyone seemed to be enjoying it so much.

Rose sang with the rest. Sam noticed that and glanced down at the words. They reminded him of what Rose had said the other night about blood sacrifices. That had bothered him a little when he thought about it. Maybe she had something. But he had tried not to give it too much thought.

There were more songs, a prayer, and finally the young man started to speak. He used a conversational tone and began with a simple illustration. He had a slight accent; it might have been Scotch.

"When I was a boy," he told them, "I had to help my father tend the sheep. You don't have many sheep here in this country. Perhaps what I tell you will be new to you.

"One day a little lamb was born; but the mother died. We struggled hard to make the little thing eat. We tried medicine droppers and even a plastic sponge soaked in milk." The people smiled understandingly; they had had experience with calves. "We were afraid we would lose the lamb also. My father took her to a neighbor's nursing ewe but the mother would have nothing to do with the strange lamb. We were desperate. Then, strangely enough, the ewe's little lamb died. We thought, 'Now she will let our baby nurse.' But no, she sniffed it all over, pushed it away, and bleated for her own. At last an old shepherd came up with the answer. 'Skin the little dead lamb and tie its coat around your own lamb and ye'll have no trouble at all.' Sure enough, it worked!"

The audience had followed the homely story with rapt attention. It was right out of their own lives.

"Now let me ask you a question," went on the speaker. "What made the mother finally accept the little nursling? Because she sniffed it and it smelled like her own. Her lamb had to die to give life to the other one.

"Long ago, God gave His Son, the Lamb of God, that you and I might be wrapped in His righteousness. For we didn't *smell right to God!* We were steeped in our own works, lost in sin, ready to perish. But 'God so loved the world that He gave His only begotten Son, that whosoever believeth in Him should not perish, but have everlasting life.'"

Rose listened like a thirsty child receiving a cold drink. Tears of joy brimmed into her eyes. It was all so simple now and so reasonable. She was aware of Bill's nearness, his gaze upon her. She turned her glance up to his for an instant, and the happy tears spilled over. Frantically she pawed in her purse for a handkerchief, then she felt Bill's hand on hers and his freshly folded one was in her hand. She mopped her eyes, slipped a kiss into the clean linen, and threw him a grateful smile.

Sam wasn't looking. He was staring out the window, trying hard to think of something else than the vision of that little lamb wrapped in the skin of another.

The talk was short. There was another song, and then the preacher announced, "As is our custom, we will enjoy together the supper of our Lord. Anyone who truly loves Him is welcome to join with us."

An elderly man stepped forward to help pass the plates of bread. It was all very quiet and simple. When they came to the end of the row where Bill sat, he took a piece of bread; and Rose, looking up at him and receiving his nod, took one also. Sam was shocked. In disapproving sternness he passed the plate to the man on his right. The same thing took place when the cups of wine were served. The whole service lasted only a few minutes. There was a quiet prayer by the man seated next to Sam. It was spoken as if the Lord was right in the room with them, and it closed with the words "until He comes. Amen."

Sam couldn't wait to get out. He brushed past the usher at the door and stood leaning against the car till the others came out. They made no reference to his exit. Everyone but Sam seemed happy.

Bill looked at his watch. "We'll be at the Homestead Inn," he smiled at Rose, "just in time for dinner. It's the finest place in the world to eat. Isn't it, Rose?"

She nodded. "It's rather *dear*," she said slyly. "As I recall, our dinner was something over ten dollars, wasn't it?" She broke into a chuckle when she saw his startled expression.

"It's dear all right," he twinkled, "in more ways than one."

"Why did you do that?" she whispered archly.

"Don't you know?" he grinned. "I was paving the way for today."

She moved over a little closer to him and he reached for her hand again.

Sam sat in moody silence.

CHAPTER 16

It was Sunday night.

Dean Wittig touched the light switch beside his bed. He had read until his eyes were burning. Books were his passion. His choice was usually social study, from Socrates and Thomas More through Karl Marx, to still more modern writers. Occasionally he dabbled a little in writing himself; pamphlets usually, but never under his own name. It might have endangered his job at the college. Some day, perhaps, but it was too soon yet. He found himself constantly torn between his desire for personal success and his loyalty to the insatiable demands of the political group with which he had irrevocably allied himself.

As the light went out his telephone rang. He picked it up.

"Ray?"

"Yes, Ed."

"Did they tell you yet?"

"What?"

"I'm fired."

A long silence.

"No!"

"Yes! Now I'm going to work from the other end."

"Oh? Trouble among the students is not a pleasant prospect for a dean," growled Wittig.

"No, but we have to keep the ball rolling. It'll be up to you to clear me and get me reinstated. I'll work from my end through you know who."

Wittig frowned in displeasure.

"Keep in touch. Let me know the score."

"Okay," grumpily muttered the dean.

Edward Karpinsky put down the phone and sat in deep thought for some time. Then he looked at the clock. Eleven. Not too late. He picked up the phone again and called Holley Hall.

Verna heard the knock on the door. She poked her roommate.

"Phone call for you, Edda." She had to shake her awake.

Edda was gone several minutes, but Verna was still awake when she crawled into bed again. Verna had learned not to ask too many questions. She lay still. But she was soon aware that Edda was not falling asleep easily.

It was not long before she heard, "Verna."

Verna flopped over. "Yes?"

"I'm so mad I could pop."

"What's the matter?"

"Some moron goofed off and they've fired Karpen."

Verna leaned up on an elbow. "Fired him! What for?"

"I'm not sure. Some stupid knucklehead has criticized his views."

"It's funny he didn't say anything about it Saturday night," mused Verna.

"It just now happened. Talk about free speech! Doesn't it burn you up? Don't *you* think Karpie has the finest mind in this whole institution?" Edda sat up in bed. "We've got to do something about it! This will be our class project. We'll do some group dynamics. I talked it all over with Karpie. They can't do this to him. Now shut up and let me think."

If there was one thing that Verna was persuaded of, it was that her roommate was smart. So she was not surprised the next morning when she revealed her plan.

"We'll have no trouble except with a few isolated opinionists, squares like that Sam of yours and his big bad blond."

Verna looked troubled. Squares? Those two? Maybe she still didn't understand just what a square was.

"What are we going to do?" It didn't occur to her not to say "we."

"A sit-out," stated Edda firmly. "The majority will go along with it. That will teach the old creeps that they can't run this college. It's for students, isn't it? Not for profs. Then the students should have a voice in choosing who's going to teach them. I'd sure like to know who threw the monkey wrench." Suddenly she exclaimed, "I'll bet I do know! And I'm going to *get* him!" She whirled on Verna. "Verna Mae, you've got to stick with us or you'll *wish you had*. Understand?"

Verna nodded uncertainly.

"Okay. Don't get any notions. Obey orders. Keep your mouth shut and use your head."

Rather pleased that she was to be trusted in whatever conspiracy was afoot, Verna followed along to breakfast.

There was much lobbying to be done by Edda that morning. Political science class was the last period before lunch. Somehow word of the sit-out got around.

In spite of notices on the bulletin board and the class-room blackboard, that the class would not meet that day, practically every member arrived promptly and took their places.

Someone had made up a roll call from memory; Pinky Clapp was assigned to read it. She performed the duty, with much giggling and many wisecracks from the class. Only three names received no response of "Here": Bill Lodge, Sam Goldman, and Oliver Snead.

No one made any reference to Oliver Snead; no one ever paid any attention to whether he was there or not. He had rarely contributed to the discussions. He was a nonentity, interesting only to his books and his cameras. But when the other two were pronounced delinquent, the students were not quite sure how to take it. Then Tracy Posden, carefully primed by Edda, suggested that they should be denounced at traitors to the cause.

"After all, wasn't it Bill Lodge who handed out those crazy ideas at the beginning of the year? You couldn't expect him to be normal."

"And he was the one who talked about 'permission' to hold our last club meeting, wasn't he?"

"Sure, it's easy to guess whodunit. 'Twas a dastardly deed. Karpie was a good egg."

Edda, biding her time, was satisfied. Convinced that she had done a good job of selling, she now arose and stalked to the front of the room. She had dressed with great care; she knew how to attract attention. She opened her mouth as if to speak. Tracy and Colley, ready supporters, started shushing. When the room was quiet, she began her speech.

"I'm sure our absent Karpie would give you all A's," she announced with a confident smile and an assured toss of her sleek head. "This is true group dynamics."

Some laughed at that, some moaned, but she was for the most part well received. After all, she was the dean's niece.

"Of course we have all speculated on who was the brownie! I guess there isn't much doubt in our minds now. The absentee list speaks for itself. The question is, what to do about it. Let's remember that America *is* a free country; the majority rule. And we can constitute a majority if we'll all stick with it and insist on our rights. I suggest that we stay right here until we get action, the action we demand. This is one of the largest classes enrolled in the college. We can draft recruits from Mr. Karpen's other classes. In time we can disrupt things enough to make our voice heard effectively. A day or two and they'll have to act."

Her low, vibrant tone bespoke such authority that the plan began to seem reasonable. It sounded like a lark. No classes! A cause to champion! Limelight!

"Why, we might even be written up in the newspapers. Think what that would mean in encouraging other students to stand up for their rights. They tell us America is degenerating; that its young people are becoming soft. Let's show what we're made of; show the country we can fight!"

The strike was on. Edda was intoxicated with the success of her project. Every now and then through the rest of the day, whenever she sensed that the morale was sinking, she would make another speech, or send Tracy or some other to the front, after careful coaching.

A note was composed with care and sent to the office of the president. It demanded the reinstatement of Karpen with full rights to conduct his courses in whatever way he chose.

Excitement ran high. They were constantly in expectation of a visit from the powers that be. There were frequent chants: "We want Karpen! We want Karpen." They wasted reams of notebook paper writing speeches to be delivered in answer to the anticipated demands of the authorities that they disperse. They took turns delivering the speeches for practice.

Verna was troubled. Her first reaction, when she heard the news of Karpen's dismissal, was relief; now she would not have to do anything about that dishonest exam paper. Or would she? Somehow his absence did not clear her conscience. And now new worries were added; she was missing her other classes; also, she kept wondering why Sam was not in on the sit-out. Hadn't he heard of it? That wasn't fair to him. Surely by now he must have discovered what was going on. Why didn't he join them? She didn't know Bill very well, but she had a great deal of respect for him. Where was he? Had he really reported Mr. Karpen?

Interest began to wane toward evening. No one had appeared to dissuade them. There were whispers of anticlimax.

Just then a local newspaper man, clandestinely tipped off, was smuggled in. He questioned several and took pictures. They hid him until dark, then sent him down the back way. They settled in for the night. Rules were set up and strictly adhered to; only one person at a time was permitted to leave the room. No comforts were allowed, beyond a cushion or two that could be snatched from a chair in passing. There was much giggling and some cuddling. But in general the morale held.

Nine o'clock. It was Verna's turn to venture out a few minutes. As she passed the Student Center she saw that the door was still open and a dim light was on in the post office section. Always subconsciously hoping against hope that there would be a miraculous letter from home saying that the news about Richard was all a mistake, that the horrible tragedy had never taken place, she stopped at her box.

There was no letter, only a note scribbled on college notebook paper.

"How about a walk again last period this morning? No class. There might even be a thunderstorm! Sam."

163

The whole big empty room turned dark with her disappointment. What had she missed? More than anything in the world she wanted a talk with Sam. She had found it impossible to classify him with the type of men to whom Edda Wittig had introduced her. Somehow she always felt clean and sane after being with him.

She had never been able to warm up to Rose; although she admired her tremendously. Rose was another girl, a girl who was not square, who knew how to dress and how to talk. She could not pour out her heart to Rose; she was a little afraid of her. Sam was different. He had been her first friend. He never seemed to condemn her. If she had only stopped here this morning! She had not been happy in that sit-out meeting all day, and she was not looking forward to a night of it. For one thing, she was still a little fearful lest Colley would try to get fresh with her again. He had avoided her since they had been back at school, but she did not trust him.

She dragged herself out of the Center and started down the walk under the elms. Unaware of the power Edda had over her, she automatically headed for the sit-out room. It didn't occur to her that she had a perfect right to go straight to her own room and go to bed.

She dreaded the long, dull night. How had her life got so tangled? Bitterly she remembered the bright dreams her teacher had painted of gay college doings. Was the world so different since that woman's collegiate days? Perhaps. Everyone seemed to think it was changing fast. Maybe it wasn't all her fault. Yet the cheating was; it still bothered her. What had made her do that? There might be some question of the right and wrong of other pleasures she had dabbled in, things that had been under the ban all her life; but there couldn't be any question about cheating. That was the same as lying or stealing.

She heard voices behind her, men's voices. They were serious, not gay and laughing. Maybe the president or some officials were coming to disperse the class. For the first time it occurred to her to wonder if there would be punishment meted out. While she was in the classroom under the spell of Edda's will, where the rest were all in accord, it had not seemed a bad thing to do. But now that room where they were holed up seemed like a rotten spot on the campus. Her pace grew slower. Dared she take things in her own hands and not go back?

The men were close behind her now. She seemed to recognize one voice. She glanced up as they passed.

"Sam!" she cried impulsively. She was so relieved that she felt as if she were home again after a long, weary journey.

"I just now got your note, Sam. I'm very — I'm *terribly* disappointed." She sounded so pitiful that he laughed. Bill looked down at her wonderingly.

"Well, another time, maybe," said Sam pleasantly.

They started on but she called to them.

"Oh, would you wait just a minute, please? I — I've got to talk to you. I must ask you something." She lowered her voice. "Did you know what was going on in Mr. Karpen's class today?"

They nodded non-committally.

"Well, what do you think of it?" she demanded.

"I really don't know much about it," shrugged Sam.

"Tell her the truth, man," urged Bill. "It's too late to beat around the bush."

Sam looked at Bill and hesitated.

"It's no good," put in Bill boldly, without waiting for Sam. "No good at all. It's just what you could expect of that man's philosophy. It's communistic and can't lead to anything but anarchy."

Verna caught her breath in horror. "Really? Oh, I didn't know I was getting into a thing like that."

165

"Have you been in there?" Sam spoke sharply. Verna shrank from the sternness in his voice.

"Yes, till a little while ago. I thought everyone was supposed to. I wondered why neither of you were there. They read the roll; you two and that little Snead fellow were the only ones who didn't come. They were blaming you, Bill, for reporting on Mr. Karpen."

"Good! I wish I had. It would have been an honor."

"You didn't? Who did, then?"

"I don't know. But whoever it was deserves a medal."

"Well, I won't go back there, that's sure," decided Verna.

"You will be very wise not to. If they escape being suspended or even expelled they will be fortunate."

Verna looked frightened.

"Who seems to be the leading spirit?" persisted Bill.

"Why, I guess you'd say my roommate, Edda Wittig. She has made a lot of speeches. She had a telephone call late last night. I think it was Mr. Karpen. She came back very angry, and she lay awake a long time planning this."

Sam and Bill looked at each other and nodded. "Just what I'd expect," said Sam. "Look, VeeEm, you've been running around a lot lately with that Wittig girl, haven't you? Why?"

"Well, she's my roommate, you know." Verna hesitated. She was evidently keeping something back.

"That's not it, VeeEm. Out with it."

She gave a desperate, pitiful look at him and then at Bill. Obviously she didn't feel as free to talk before him.

"Look, VeeEm," Sam urged, "you aren't like you used to be. And that female dreadnaught is not helping you any."

"But Sam, you said yourself I was a square, and she promised to help me rub the corners off. She has

166

really been nice to me. She taught me to do my hair, and gave me clothes and things and even took me to New York over the holidays." Verna suddenly realized that it was an invitation to Sam's home that she had turned down for the New York trip. But he paid no attention to that.

"VeeEm, you need a good lecture. Yes, you were square. But you're just as square this way. It doesn't become you. You aren't Edda Wittig and be thankful you're not. Don't try to be like her. Look, you gave out once that you were on the Lord's side. Why don't you act like it?"

"Oh." Verna's balloon collapsed.

"Now I'll tell you what to do. We've been reviewing this whole deal. There is more to it than meets the eye. Go on back to the dorm tonight and go to your regular classes in the morning. If there isn't any political science class meet me in the post office. We'll go somewhere and have a chit-chat. If there is a class we'll make it later. And *don't talk! Not to anyone.* Get me?"

"Yes," she agreed. "Oh, I'm so glad you turned up here."

The boys departed and she started on toward Holley Hall. But she hadn't gone ten steps when a healthy iron grip seized her arm and whirled her around. She started to scream.

"Okay, double crosser!" growled a familiar, hateful voice. Colley's other hand covered her mouth. He was propelling her swiftly toward the little back entrance to the main classroom building where the sit-out was going on. She struggled and kicked him.

"You wildcat! I swore I'd get you some time." He freed her mouth in order to pick her up and carry her. She screamed again and tried to claw at his face. He held her tighter so that she could scarcely breathe. She thought her eyes would pop out of her head.

"You two-faced biddy! Thought you'd double-cross

167

your best friend. We saw you from up there. Yes," as she gasped and struggled, "you forgot there's a little back window in that room, didn't you? Well, you'll learn. You've got a lot to — "

His words choked off into silence and Verna suddenly felt herself free. Colley was sprawling on the grass, rolling over on Sam. He raised his great fist and struck with all his might. His left got Sam in the stomach and his mighty right hit him on the head. Sam groaned, struggling in vain to get on his feet.

Colley rose, swearing, to make another dive for Verna. But before he knew it he was hurled through the air. He landed on the concrete sidewalk. Bill stood over him ready to handle him if he still showed signs of renewing the fight. But he lay inert.

Verna was on her knees beside Sam. Bill stooped over him.

"How bad are you hurt, old man?"

With Bill's help Sam managed to get to his feet, but he couldn't speak. There was blood coming from his mouth. He put his hand to his head and moaned.

"Get in there quick," Bill commanded Verna, pointing to the dorm. "Tell your house mother to call the infirmary, and have the doc there. I'll get Sam over right away. Then we'll come back for Corbett. You better stay out of it."

Bill slung Sam's arm over his shoulder and started off; Sam's legs were stumbling and dragging pitifully.

Wild-eyed, Verna appeared at Mrs. Ross's door.

"They want you to call the infirmary. Sam's hurt. Get the doctor there. And Colley Corbett, too," she added, but it seemed at the moment that no one mattered but Sam.

Mrs. Ross hobbled to the phone, with calm efficiency made the call, then buzzed Rose's room.

"Now you said Colley Corbett. I am to call him, too? What for?"

"Oh no," stammered Verna. "He was hurt, badly.

Or — " A horrid thought occurred to her. "Maybe he's *dead!*" She tore out again.

Mrs. Ross limped hippety-hopping after her. What had her stormy little freshman been up to? She was sure that it must have something to do with the sit-out. She had been told of it, of course. She knew that eight or ten of her girls were not in their rooms. The administration, strongly influenced by the dean, had been inclined to treat it lightly. They had decided to let it go for a few hours, until ten o'clock, and then if the students had not tired of their game, the president himself would go in and sternly order them all to bed, to appear before the authorities in the morning. The dean advised him that he considered it a prank. Mrs. Ross, knowing Edda, was concerned, but of course she had no authority to act.

She found Verna scanning the ground frantically.

"He isn't here!" said the distraught girl in a hollow toneless whisper.

"Tell me what happened," ordered Mrs. Ross with unwonted sternness.

Verna opened her mouth, stared at her, closed it again and took off like a frightened rabbit.

Mrs. Ross took her troubled, bobbling way back to the dorm. Rose was waiting, in answer to her buzz. She took one look at the woman's distressed face.

"What is wrong?" she cried.

"I wish I knew." Mrs. Ross picked up the phone and dialed. "I'm calling Dr. Barnett. But you had better check with the infirmary. Verna burst in here with a tall tale about Sam's being hurt. I don't know whether the child is out of her mind or not. I ordered her to explain but she ran off."

Rose, white-lipped, was already at the door.

She ran all the way to the small building set apart for first aid and minor ills. The doctor's car was parked in front.

She opened the door softly.

CHAPTER 17

Colley stirred and gave his head a shake. There was quite a lump on the back of it. He sat up dizzily. Then it all came back to him. Edda had sent him down to get Verna and Sam had come along and grabbed him by surprise. His pal Bill — the dirty skunk! — must have been sneaking around somewhere and used judo on him. No one could beat Colley Corbett in a fair fight. Where were they all?

He staggered to his feet. Had to get back up there or they'd think he was a punk. On the way upstairs to the sit-out he did some fast thinking.

He felt his way along the dark corridor and entered the room. His head ached frightfully.

An air of confusion pervaded the place. Morale was low. The injured innocence plank in Edda's platform was splintering in places.

"Where is she?" whispered Edda, at Colley's side the instant he opened the door.

"Search me," he replied angrily. "When I got down there that kike was with her there in the dark so I gave him the old one-two and tried to grab her and get her up here safely. But I guess she ran home when I pulled him away from her."

Edda lit a cigarette and gave him a long look in the light of her match. "I saw it all," she said significantly. He could barely hear her. "Okay, we'll get him."

Within half an hour every member of the sit-out band had retreated at the mild persuasion of Dean Wittig who was summoned by Colley himself at Edda's order. With sober precision he took the names of those present and pacifically ordered them to meet in his office in the morning.

"It was appeasement, pure and simple," announced Edda to her cohorts. "That means we have won a point. We can push it farther if we like. As far as I am concerned this college would be a waste of time without Karpen's stimulating mind." The rest gave tacit agreement but there was more than one troubled pillow that night. Absentees from their other classes were sure to draw F's.

Edda gave last instructions to Tracy and Colley before they separated. "Now for our next move, I think we should see that the real blame for the whole disturbance is placed where it belongs. You heard Uncle Raymond explain that there have been complaints of subversive activity. I think there's no question of its source, is there?" She glared as if she dared them to contradict. "Tracy, you still have the record of those club meetings, haven't you? Yes," she took his notebook and scanned it, "here it is, in black and white, and we all heard it. You might know who would be at the bottom of it. Sam Goldman made a suggestion right in the meeting that the 'basic fundamentals of the constitution' be amended. Remember?" she insisted. "Perhaps," went on the leader self-righteously, "we have done wrong in not reporting this. When my uncle realizes who the real un-American culprit is, Karpie may be recalled before we know it."

They parted for the night to enjoy the peaceful slumber due true patriots.

Mrs. Ross had not yet located Verna when Rose returned. The other girls had come in from the sit-out and gone sheepishly up to bed, all except Edda Wittig. Mrs. Ross had been inclined to give them a good lecture then and there, but she was not sure yet what stand the administration was planning to take on the affair. She had not been able to reach either President Barnett or the dean on the phone. Her own decision would have been suspension at least. But for the time being she simply gave the girls stern looks and listed their names as they slunk off upstairs.

Just as Rose was about to lock the door for the night, Edda slid in. She gave Rose a scornful, defiant glance and started to sail off to her room. Mrs. Ross called her.

Disapproval showed through her usual calm. "Edda, have you seen your roommate? She is not yet in."

Edda gave a mocking laugh. "No, I haven't. She left my loving care." She turned and faced Rose. Staring her up and down insultingly, she sneered, "Maybe your brother knows where she is." Then she stalked off down the corridor to the stairway, her heels stabbing the floor at every step.

Rose flushed and bit her lip. Even Mrs. Ross was indignant. She spoke severely, "Let me know immediately, Edda, if Verna turns up." But Edda had other work to do before she went to bed.

The house mother signalled Rose to come into her own living room.

"Don't be too disturbed over that girl," she advised. "I've never breathed this before, but between you and me," Mrs. Ross leaned toward Rose and whispered, "she's a brat. She takes advantage of the fact that her uncle is the dean." Mrs. Ross put her hands gently on Rose's shoulders and studied her. To her surprise the girl managed a trembling smile.

"I'm not — upset," she said. "You see, I — have been learning a lot — since Saturday." Her beautiful, limpid, dark eyes wavered and dropped, then she looked up bravely. "You will be glad. I know Jesus Christ now. He is my Saviour, too."

Mrs. Ross folded her warmly in her arms. "Praise the Lord! You precious child."

Rose smiled; her new-found peace was in her eyes. "I'm so glad I found Him, or rather, He found me — before all this happened. I have the strangest sense tonight that He knows about Sam's being hurt, and all, and He will take care of us." She drew a deep breath.

"Of course He does," agreed Mrs. Ross. "Now, sit down and tell me all you know about what has happened."

"That isn't much. I saw Sam at the infirmary only a moment. Doc Agee took him to the hospital over on the main line. He's badly hurt; he couldn't talk. The nurse didn't know how it happened. The doctor said it may be concussion; his jaw is broken." She put her head down on the older woman's shoulder and shook with weary dry sobs.

Mrs. Ross held the girl close. Fear of the unknown was in their eyes.

When Edda reached the second floor, she went down the hall to the telephone and called the president's home.

"Dr. Barnett," she said in a sweet muffled tone, "this is Edda Wittig. I couldn't say anything to my uncle in the classroom when all the kids were there, but I think you should know that there's more to all this than just our monkeyshines." She paused to be sure of a sympathetic ear at the other end of the line. Reassured, she continued.

"There is a certain Semitic member of our class who needs to be investigated. I think you may guess who I mean. His sister works here in the dorm. We have proof that he is the subversive element. He may even be actually involved with communist agents; he has certainly made some statements in class which are un-American, to say the least. We can show you one of them, in the minutes of our meeting. We all heard it. I thought you ought to know before we see you tomorrow. No, he was not with us today. He doesn't go along with the class as a whole, usually. I guess that's enough proof, isn't it, that our sit-out was on the level? Honestly, we do think a lot of Mr. Karpen. That's all we're fighting for, to have him back. Some

173

of us have wondered if it wasn't this Jew's activities that sparked your informer's suspicions. All right, sir, I'm glad to get it off my mind. I know you will take care of it. Thank you, Dr. Barnett. Good night."

With righteous complacency she took her way up the other flight of stairs and after visiting two or three carefully selected rooms and chatting a few minutes in the dark in each, she sought a hard earnest rest. She smiled back at her own clever green eyes in the crooked mirror of the bathroom.

When Bill returned and found no prostrate Colley, he raced across campus to the men's dorm, up the stairs three at a time, and burst into the room the four fellows occupied together. There was Oliver Snead, puttering as usual with his camera equipment. His math book lay open on his desk. His too large glasses had slipped partway down his too small nose. He looked like a discouraged owl.

"Corbett been here the last few minutes?" Bill panted.

Oliver shook his head. "I don't know how he ekth-peckth to path. He never thtudieth." He said it wistfully as if he wished he could manage with so little effort.

Bill disappeared before he had finished his last sentence, and Oliver continued to fuss with his camera.

Bill made the rounds, tearing from classroom to infirmary. No one anywhere. It was a good quarter of a mile from the infirmary to the men's dorm, so he could have missed everyone all the way around. At last he called Rose.

"Oh, Bill! I'm so glad you called." Mrs. Ross pricked up her ears at Rose's lilt of glad relief.

"Do you know how Sam is?" he asked anxiously.

She told him what she knew. "Bill, do you know *what* happened tonight? It's all so very mysterious."

Bill hesitated. "Yes, I do. I was there." He paused. "You sound mysterious, too. What *is* going on?"

174

"Well, I think maybe I oughtn't to let it spread around campus. This is a public phone. There's nothing for you to worry about; that is, if Sam is not hurt too badly. I'll tell you all about it tomorrow. It's quite a tale."

"But Verna has disappeared."

"She has!" ejaculated Bill in alarm.

"Yes. Mrs. Ross asked her what happened and she wouldn't tell her a thing; just stared at her. And now we can't find her anywhere. The girls have all been in a quarter of an hour ago. Verna is never late."

"I'll go right out and look for her. Corbett's disappeared, too. I don't like that. If I don't find her in half an hour I'll call you."

Rose put up the phone with a troubled frown. Bill sounded really alarmed. She went to Mrs. Ross.

"There's something peculiar underneath all this," she insisted. "I feel as if we were on the verge of some terrible calamity."

Mrs. Ross did not smile or try to talk her out of her fears. "There are lots of peculiar things going on in the world," she agreed. "Some are real and some aren't. Let's just talk to the Lord about it, shall we? He knows the whole situation, and we can trust Sam and Verna, too, in His hands. Oh, it is going to be good to have you understand and be able to pray with me!" She gave Rose a loving caress.

It was a new experience for Rose, kneeling there in the quiet, hearing her friend pour out her heart in confident supplication and praise to One whom she seemed to know well.

She offered a stumbling petition herself, and wondered why she felt such a rush of gladness in the midst of all the uncertainties.

As she rose from her feet she apologized shyly, "I don't know very well yet how to pray."

"My darling girl," smiled Mrs. Ross, "let me tell you something that I remember from long ago. When

175

our one little girl was born, there was nothing sweeter to us than her baby-talk. Don't you think our Heavenly Father must feel the same way?"

"Oh, you make it so wonderful!" exclaimed Rose.

"Not nearly so wonderful as it really is."

"But I never knew you had a daughter."

"You will meet her some day. She stayed with us only two years. Then the Lord took her Home, just after my husband went." Mrs. Ross smiled and sighed as if in anticipation.

Rose watched her in wonder. "How different everything seems when you know you can count on Him!"

Mrs. Ross took Rose's lovely face between her soft hands and kissed her. "You don't know how wonderful it is to me to feel that I have a daughter again, in you," she said. They were standing in the dim light in Rose's room which she occupied alone, across the hall from Mrs. Ross.

Suddenly they were startled by hearing a click on the window pane. They waited. Then another click. Rose went to the window. A voice called in a stage whisper, "Rose! Rose! Let me in, please. I didn't know it was so late."

She put up the window cautiously. It was Verna.

"Come around to the front door, honey," she told her.

"I think I'll just go in my room and leave her to you," suggested the house mother. "It may be she will talk to you. Don't scold her for being late." Rose nodded and went to let the girl in.

Verna had been crying. For the first time since she came to school and upset her tray in the dining room, she had allowed her tears to get the upper hand of her.

"Where on earth have you been, honey? We've been looking everywhere for you. Are you all right?" Rose put a loving arm about her.

"Yes, I'm all right," returned Verna in a small

176

frightened voice. "I've been up on the rock behind the dorm." Her voice broke and she seemed near to giving away again. Rose drew her into her own room and closed the door.

"What was wrong, honey? Tell me about it." It did not occur to Rose that just a few short weeks ago she had felt utterly inadequate to deal with this girl. Now it seemed as natural as comforting a sister.

But Verna wouldn't talk. She merely sat still with a woe-begone expression, and shook her head.

Finally Rose asked her, "Well, maybe you will tell me *why* you won't talk?" She spoke very gently as if she were coaxing a young wild faun from the forest.

In a voice scarcely audible Verna answered her despairingly, "Because Sam told me not to."

"Sam!" exclaimed Rose in amazement.

"Yes. He said not to talk to anyone, that he would see me tomorrow. Oh, Rose is he going to be all right?" She was frantic with anxiety. "Was he hurt terribly? I peeked in the infirmary window but I couldn't hear what they said. And Bill said to stay out of it."

"He's hurt, and he may have a concussion."

"Oh-h!" she moaned.

Rose waited, wondering what her next move should be. Then Verna burst out,

"What happened to Colley? Is he — dead?"

"We don't know where he is yet. He — " Then the phone rang. Rose hurried to answer it, leaving Verna trembling on the couch in an effort to still her apprehensions.

It was Bill. "That shiftless scoundrel Corbett is here in bed asleep," he announced. "But I can't find hide nor hair of your girl."

"She just came in. She's terribly upset over something and she won't talk. She says Sam told her not to."

Bill thought a moment. "Oh! I know." He laughed.

177

"I'm glad there's *some*thing to laugh at," wailed Rose,

"Well, there is, a little, although I'm still burnt up. I'll tell you tomorrow. Let the kid alone tonight and we'll take her over to see Sam tomorrow. He'll straighten her out."

Relieved, Rose went back to her room. But when she tried to get Verna to go to bed, the poor girl started to shake all over with nervous apprehension. "I won't go up there again. Not with Edda. I'd rather stay outdoors all night. I can't face her. I don't know *what* she'd do to me. She told me not to talk, too."

Puzzled, Rose decided not to force the issue.

"All right. You can stay right here and sleep on my couch. See? It's plenty wide enough. You go take a nice warm bath and I'll lend you a nightie. We'll put the whole thing out of our minds until tomorrow."

Rose was touched at the grateful look Verna gave her. Hesitantly the poor girl took the things she offered and obeyed. Soothed by the bath, she crept into the bed Rose had made up on her couch, and soon she was fast asleep. Rose kept an eye on her, and when she was sure that Verna was off for the night, she slid across the hall to consult with Mrs. Ross.

CHAPTER 18

Dean Wittig was puzzled.

Dr. Barnett had phoned him about Edda's call, and it had confused him. That was one thing he always disliked about intelligence work. Agents spied on agents who were spying on agents. He was not sure he could trust Edda's information or her judgment, yet what if she were right? Of course she didn't know what it meant to him. Or did she? Who knew whom to trust? Everything was so secretive.

He got out Sam's file and went over it. Sure enough, he had worked for a while on a newspaper that covered that affair two years ago when Ed Karpinsky had been on the spot. That was almost proof positive that Sam was here for a reason. It must be that Ed was spotted. Maybe he was himself, but that he doubted. If he played the game well, he should be safe.

But that Lodge fellow. The dean was well aware of his intimacy with Goldman. He gave Bill's record, also, a thorough sifting. Bill had asked for a Jewish roommate; he must have had this one in mind. Could he possibly have been sent by Washington to watch him? Or was Goldman himself spying on Karpen? The two boys roomed with that Snead character. That also clicked. Bill must be the one who had put Snead up to reporting Karpen. Young Snead was not smart enough to suspect anything. If Lodge was from C.I.A. he would have been given a dossier with all the information about his roommates and their family connections.

Now, what to do about it? He sat for several hours through the night playing an imaginary chess game, trying out certain moves, reasoning out counter moves. There were always his original orders that had to be considered, and strict rules. But that made the game all the more challenging.

It was nearly four o'clock when he decided on his course. Even then he did not sleep well, and the telephone woke him at seven. It was New York calling. He was alert at once. Karpen! This could mean more trouble and a change of plans. But it was only the manager of his brother's apartment building. George Wittig was under oxygen in the hospital with a heart attack. He might not live out the day.

Raymond Wittig was annoyed rather than shocked. He sat for some minutes evaluating the effect that this might have on his own life, if any. Finally he called Holley Hall and asked for Edda.

"I want you over here right away." He spoke more sternly than usual; since the sit-out he had the whip hand over his niece, and he intended to make the most of it. He never felt easy with her around; she was too smart. He knew that the college board would be enough for him to reckon with at present. Edda might turn out to be in the know after all, but until he was sure he would rather handle the sit-out minus her leadership.

"Oh, Uncle Raymond, have a heart," whined Edda, only half awake.

"Now!" he ordered. "Right away."

"Okay, okay!" she muttered. He had already hung up. "You might think I had done something criminal." For once she missed Verna; there was no one to scold.

Her uncle's place was only a block off campus. She arrived promptly.

"Well, let's have it," she demanded abruptly.

Her uncle was like her. He did not waste words. "Your father is in the hospital," he told her bluntly. "Heart attack. He may not live. I think you had better go. There's a plane in an hour. I got you a seat. I'll have one of the workmen drive you over."

In typical Wittig style, Edda quickly re-arranged her cards to see how to play. What would affect her own interests? Her green eyes narrowed.

"Okay, I'll go." She spoke laconically. "But I can get someone to drive me. You needn't bother."

"Suit yourself. You have money?"

"Yes. Just give me a break on my classes. Do we get Karpen back?"

"Um - uh - possibly, later. At present I shall take the class myself."

Edda whisked out, called the men's dorm and sent for Tracy.

"It's too bad," she told him, on the way to the airport, "my being away while all this is going on. But just go along, all of you, with what *they* want, and I think we'll get what *we* want in time. I had a talk with my uncle. The big scoop today will be Goldman's attack on the little Dutch square. To think that he's a communist! You never know. It burns me up, especially when I remember what he said once about you."

"Me?" Tracy bridled at once, as she had meant he should.

"Yes, you! Never mind, I don't want to make things any worse than they are between you. Well, thanks for the lift. I'll do something for you sometime."

"That's okay. I hope your father—"

"My father? Oh, George'll make the grade. He always has." She waved a careless good-by from the ramp of the plane.

By the time Tracy returned from the airport the news of Sam's inexcusable assault on the innocent young freshman was all over the campus, and Colley Corbett was a hero. Tracy heard it and shrugged. "Well, so what?" he said to himself. "I'm certainly not going to bat for Sam."

"Did you hear about that Sam Goldman?" hissed Pinky Clapp across her tray at the breakfast table.

Joan Denison cocked a pink ear. "No, what?" She was not one whom Edda had visited. "I think he's neat. Those black eyes of his make me simply swoon. I've tried since that very first day on the train to make him look at me. I think he's a woman hater."

"Woman hater like crazy. Wait till you hear." Pinky lowered her tones. "It seems that country Dutch freak Schiffelgruber was on her way back to the sit-out last night and he . . ." her voice sank to a succulent whisper. "Can you imagine? He sure picked one. And you know she's such a pious Polly. Well, she *screamed!* Isn't that quaint? If she had any sense she'd have welcomed a little romance. She'll never get any, any other way. Just then our big hero Colley Corbett turns up, rescues the damsel and half slays the dirty villain. Talk about corny westerns!"

All day rumors flew fast. The whole campus was hot with them. As they spread they varied:

Sam Goldman was a communist agent; Bill Lodge was a government man set to watch him.

Sam Goldman was wanted by the FBI; Verna had been primed to waylay him.

Colley Corbett was also a government man, hired to guard both Verna and Bill.

Bill, unaware of Corbett's role, had mistakenly attacked Corbett.

Mr. Karpen was an innocent bone of contention, loved by loyal, patriotic students, especially Edda Wittig; maligned by those who were red-tinged, especially Sam Goldman.

FBI agents were on Campus at this moment, investigating. Sam might be apprehended as soon as he was out of the hospital.

Pinky was the first to inform Rose. She waylaid her in the lounge of the dorm where she was straightening up.

"Rosie!" she accosted her sympathetically. "Is it really true that the FBI are waiting for your brother to get well so they can arrest him? I think that's foul! It's getting so no one can open their mouths even in college where we're supposed to have academic freedom. I'm sure your brother didn't mean anything much by what he said in that meeting. I was there. And it seems to me he's going to have enough trouble about this picklement with the Dutch girl and all, without having intelligence men on his trail. I wouldn't worry about it, if I were you. But do let me know if there's anything I can do to help you. I'll take your work for you awhile, you know, if you have to go to court for him or something. 'By. Hope everything comes out all right."

If Pinky had handed her a time bomb Rose couldn't have been more stunned. She stood speechless where Pinky had met her, a pile of magazines from the coffee table in her hand. Mrs. Ross came out of her room and found her so, minutes later, staring into space, her face as white as paper.

Mrs. Ross led her gently to a couch and sat down beside her.

"Tell me, dear. What is it?"

With an effort Rose brought her eyes slowly back to the other woman's face. She shook her head slowly and made the sound of a wordless moan. Mrs. Ross took her cold hand and held it in a firm warm grasp.

"Talk, dear," she commanded. "It will help. Just pour it all out. Remember that whatever it is, the Lord knows all about it and He has a way out."

The tears started at that. "That's just it," wailed Rose, catching her breath in sobs. "I told Him last night that I wanted to be His, *all* His, for Him to do with as He wanted. I didn't think it would be—like this!"

Her hand went up to her mouth as if to steady its trembling.

"It's—my brother," she stammered. "They're saying terrible things about him. They're not true. I know Sam. They're not true."

"Of course not," agreed Mrs. Ross in a matter-of-fact tone. "That's a great deal to be thankful for, isn't it?"

A glimmer of a smile tried to break through on Rose's face. "I—I suppose it is. Yes, of course. But Mrs. Ross, how *could* they accuse our Sam of being communistic? It's impossible. He *hates* anything like that."

"Some enemy is at work, Rose." Mrs. Ross struggled to find any items in her mind that would even begin to explain the motive for such an accusation. "And when there are enemies fighting us, we mustn't collapse. Perk up now, and we'll ask the Lord to fight for us, and show us what to do."

"But there was more. Something about last night and Verna. I was so stunned I didn't even ask any more about it. I remember now that even Bill sort of implied that there was something disgraceful. He wouldn't tell it over the phone."

"Where is Verna?"

"She is in class now. At least I guess she is. She slept well and seemed better this morning. But she still wouldn't talk. I decided not to try to force her. We'll take her over to see Sam this afternoon. He could scarcely speak last night."

"She seemed afraid of Edda, didn't she? I have a feeling that girl is at the bottom of this trouble somehow."

"Edda signed out this morning early to go to New York. She said her father was very ill and Dean Wittig advised her to go. I checked with him."

"I'm glad you did. It looks very strange, her slipping out of the picture just now. But perhaps I'm misjudging her. Poor Verna. If she gets wind of this I'm afraid it will finish her."

When Bill caught the rumors darting around the campus on Tuesday morning, he was inclined to want to fight everyone he talked to. The newspaper had the whole story of the sit-out, with pictures. After two or three bouts of attempting to get the real truth across, he hunted up Rose.

She was tearfully grateful to see him. "Now at last maybe you'll tell me what happened," she pleaded. But he looked grim.

"Let's go out to the Homestead for lunch," he suggested. "You've heard the tales, I take it?"

She nodded.

"I don't think either of us will relish any food here today."

"I told Verna we would take her over to the hospital to see Sam. She's in pretty bad shape. As soon as she heard the gossip about her and Sam this morning she

184

skipped her classes and took refuge in her room. She still won't talk."

"Maybe we ought to take her along to lunch."

Rose's eyes shone. That was just like her Bill. She felt deeply sympathetic toward the forlorn freshman.

"I'd like it to be just us," he said, "but she has no one."

"I'll call her," she said.

Verna was pathetically pleased.

"It's right on our way," explained Rose. "We can go across country to the hospital after lunch."

It was good to get out into the brightness of the country. Tears and gossip had dimmed the beauty of the campus for the time being.

When their orders were taken, Bill said, "VeeEm, you deserve a medal. I heard Sam tell you not to talk. It's not many women who could be trusted to keep their mouths shut like that. I congratulate you."

The poor girl was so astonished to be praised instead of blamed for not talking that she gazed at him in amazement. She had to struggle with tears of relief.

"They've all made it rough for you, haven't they? Someone deliberately started this lying campaign. I'm going to find out who it was if it's my last act."

He began at the beginning and told Rose the incident on the campus walk in detail. Verna kept nodding in agreement.

"Did Colley hurt you?" asked Rose with concern.

Verna forgot her vow of silence.

"No," she said thoughtfully. "I believe he was only trying to get me to go back to the sit-out. But I—I was afraid of him. Once, he got—well, awfully fresh!" She shuddered again at the memory. "Oh," she moaned softly, "I don't even want to go back to college. It was *horrible* today. Everyone looked at me and made remarks. Why did I ever come here?"

She was so near to tears again that Bill quickly changed the subject to Sam.

"Take it easy, VeeEm." He had adopted the name he had heard his roommate use so often. "We don't want to upset Sam."

At the hospital they found Sam feeling better; his jaw was wired together and very painful, but the danger of concussion was past. Verna couldn't keep her eyes from him. They kept fluttering back as often as she would tear them away. Bill and Rose both noticed it, but they decided that Sam was oblivious.

Bill tried to cheer them all up by a little teasing.

"Well, Sam, I'll have to hand it to you; you have taught one woman how to keep her mouth shut."

Sam didn't feel much like talking, and he couldn't smile, but he winked at Verna. Then he took his pencil and wrote:

"Confucius say, Speech is silver but silence is Goldman."

Soberly he tore it off and handed it to Bill who groaned and gave it to the girls. They giggled appreciatively. Then Sam wrote again. This sheet he handed to Verna.

"The time has come, the Walrus said, *to talk . . .*"

His eyes laughed with her as she read it.

Unused as she was to pleasantry, she glanced up cautiously to make sure how to take it. Then her face lit up with unexpected brilliance. Rose was astonished at how lovely she was when she was happy.

"Well, old man," laughed Bill, "you sure don't have anything the matter with your head!" Sam tried again to grin but gave it up. As they left, Bill took Sam's hand in his enormous grip.

"Doc says you gotta stay quiet here tonight. We may drop over tomorrow to get you. We're prayin' for you, man."

Verna watched her opportunity to slip back a moment alone with Sam.

"I don't know how to thank you," she told him, the tears brimming up in her eyes. "I was afraid maybe

186

you—" her lip trembled— "you didn't like me—for going to that sit-out."

He gazed up at her in surprise. "Skip it, VeeEm," he mumbled through shut teeth. "Glad you're okay."

She smiled and dashed out, but not before one of those tears ran over and down her flaming cheek. She mopped it hastily. Sam was reminded of the first time he saw that happen. She was a tender-hearted kid. She sort of made a fellow feel good inside.

On the way back Verna was as silent for awhile as she had been before. She was wondering over Bill's last words to his friend. What made him so different? She could not picture her brothers promising to pray for anyone. It was not only Bill's culture. There was a radiance, a steady confident joy about him all the time. Her brothers had been taught the Bible all their lives, but this man seemed to know the Lord personally and count on Him. That must be the difference. She wondered how it came about.

"Who else did you say was absent from the sit-out, Verna?"

"That funny little — " Verna caught herself and bit her lip. "I mean that real small fellow who wears glasses. He sits in the back row."

Bill chuckled. "He's a funny little fellow all right. What were you going to call him?"

Verna squirmed a little. "Well, he always reminds me of what Dryden called 'an unfeathered red two-legged thing.'" Bill and Rose roared. "But I'm ashamed of myself." She sobered. "I know how terrible it feels to be laughed at."

Bill broke off his hilarity. "I reckon you're right," he said. "But isn't there a difference between mockery and discernment?"

Verna thought that over. "Perhaps so," she sighed.

"If we cut out all keen characterization of people, ourselves included, we'd miss a lot of fun I believe God meant us to have. I think it's the people who

187

make fun of Him, or who laugh at others self-righteously that deserve the whipping post."

"You make things look so differently, so *right,*" she
said, looking at Bill thoughtfully. She was still too
much in awe of him to call him anything but "you."
"I was brought up to feel that God didn't intend for
us to have fun, that is was sort of wrong."

Rose glanced up at her lover proudly, delighting in
his wide grin and the confident answer she knew he
would be able to give.

"What about 'at Thy right hand there are pleasures
forevermore'?" He smiled eagerly.

Verna's somber eyes grew wide. "I never heard that.
Where is it?"

"At the end of the sixteenth Psalm. Oh, He's a
wonderful God. He has planned things for His children that we can't even dream of, but we don't half
trust Him. He'll work out this gossip bit, you'll see.
It will all disappear one of these days, like a fog.
God has a tomorrow for everyone of His children
that is so bright we can't even look at it yet." He
gave a brilliant smile. Rose looked up at him adoringly.

"I guess that's the only way to look at tomorrow
these days and not go crazy," she said, thinking of the
imminence of trouble for her people in Israel.

"Hasn't there always been a tomorrow?" put in
Verna. "Haven't people always sort of dreaded what
was coming? I know my folks have always talked
so fearfully of what *might* happen, like poor crops,
or illness and hospital bills. I can hear my father yet,
arguing with my oldest brother about whether it would
be better to put their profits from the farm into im-
proving the equipment or buying insurance. And I
know my grandmother has put away I don't know
how much money lest she be helpless in her old age.
She won't spend it yet and she's eighty. I've often
wondered when she thinks old age starts!" Verna spoke

rapidly and with confidence. Bill and Rose glanced at each other in surprise.

Bill continued her thought. "People used to push off the idea of the final Tomorrow, a vague two or three thousand — or even a million — years. Now that it's upon us, everyone is terrified. They're all writing books about it, and acting it on TV, yet they're afraid to discuss it in ordinary conversation."

Rose was listening intently. She spoke up with considerable vehemence. "I noticed that!" she broke in excitedly. "Even before I was — before I knew Christ and saw things so differently, I used to wonder why people always talked about total war as if it would always be in the other hemisphere. They knew it was hanging over us, too. It seemed to darken every conversation, but it was always unspoken. If anyone had dared to mention it openly, they would have been stared at as if they had made an awful *faux pas*. Why do you think that is, Bill?"

Bill considered. "Do you s'pose it's because the real Tomorrow *is* almost here and everyone knows it? Like a TV play where a crew is trapped in a submarine. The men know there's only so much air, to last only so long. They all glance at the clock, but they try not to let anyone see them doing it. That would be to admit fear. They don't know exactly what minute the end will come, but they all are aware of it, constantly. Everything, everywhere is spiraling toward a crash. Business, banks, governments, even churches. Kings and captains, slaves and freemen are all frightened together. They're building underground shelters, just as the Apostle John said they would, to 'hide themselves in dens and caves in the earth.'" He paused. "It makes you long to tell them about the one Hiding Place."

"It seems as if tomorrow means different things to different people, doesn't it?" went on Verna thoughtfully. "I think that to a lot of middle-aged people it means sickness and uselessness and penniless boredom."

"Yes, and to most teenagers it's the 'big change.' Careers and success, or — marriage," added Rose wistfully. "At least it used to be. But now it's nuclear war. I think a lot of kids now feel 'What's the use? We'll all be blown up before long, so why bother?'"

"What do *you* think?" Verna directed her question straight to Bill.

"My 'think' wouldn't amount to a hill of beans," he answered. "I only know what the Bible says. To Christians, tomorrow means the 'blessed hope,' the return of the Lord to take us to be with Him. To Gentiles, that is, the world in general, it will mean awful judgments and the collapse of civilization as we know it. To Jews — " He paused and looked down at Rose's intense face. She seemed to be hanging on his next words — "it will mean, first, the terrible time of 'Jacob's Trouble.' Israel will be attacked; Jerusalem will be besieged; the youngsters will be actually sold for money."

Rose gave a smothered scream. "Our cousins!" she cried.

"But those who put their trust in the Lord will be saved," smiled Bill reassuringly. "Then will come the tomorrow of a thousand years when Jesus Christ will rule this earth in righteousness."

"How did you learn all that?" cried Verna tensely. "I used to hear those things mentioned in church, but it was all so confused. No one seemed to really know what they meant, not even the preacher."

"It was a Jew who had become a Christian who taught me, last year. It's all very simple and clear, in the Bible, if you know where to look for it."

Rose snuggled a little closer to him. "Do you suppose you could teach it to another Jew who has become a Christian?" Her face was still white with the dread of what might be coming.

Verna stole an amazed look at her.

"I sure could! And I will."

"I want to learn it *soon!*" Rose said with desperation. "I must be able to tell my folks and really *show* it to them — if they'll listen. I guess tomorrow is almost here."

There was a catch in her voice. She didn't mention the almost daily letters from her parents, heartbreaking pleas to reconsider her Christian stand. Bill guessed more than she expressed.

"Yes," he agreed. "It's almost 'midnight.'"

Rose heaved a deep sigh as she climbed out of the car. "I can't seem to relax," she said mournfully. "I wish Sam's name were cleared. All day people have looked at me sidewise and then turned to whisper to each other. It's terrible! You'd think I'd be used to it by now. But somehow this is different."

Bill put his arm tenderly about her holding her steady. "Just remember Him! He'll take you through," he whispered gently.

She smiled up at him, but her lips were trembling.

They had drawn up in front of the entrance of Holley Hall. There on the curb, as if she were waiting for them, was Pinky Clapp. Her expression was a mixture of curiosity and contempt.

"Well, you've turned up!" she exclaimed as she passed them. "Where's Sam? You all are on the Most Wanted list, did you know it? We thought you had taken off. Has Sam escaped? Or did they get handcuffs on him?" Her frivolous mockery floated up to all the front windows of the dorm.

CHAPTER 19

To their consternation, Mrs. Ross confirmed Pinky's report. They were all summoned, each at a different hour, to meet with the president of the board.

Bill's first move was to hunt up Oliver Snead. As usual, he was at his desk; this time he was poring over calculus.

Bill drew up a chair, straddled it backwards and leaned on its back.

"Lay off a while, Snead, and give with words."

Oliver laid down his pencil, pulled down his nostrils by means of his upper lip, snuffed, and pushed up his glasses. Bill suddenly realized what a lonely life the boy must lead. His camera seemed to be his only steady companion. Bill was rather ashamed that he had been so taken up with Sam that he had rather neglected Oliver, plodding on his difficult way, alone most of the time. However, Bill could scarcely repress a twitch of his mouth at the remembrance of Verna's "unfeathered" characterization. The fellow was undoubtedly a screwball.

"What do you know about Karpen?" Bill asked point-blank.

A sly twinkle crept into the corner of Snead's eye. "Why?" he hedged.

Bill caught the twinkle with surprise. "Aha! You were the hero who reported him. Bully for you, Snead. I didn't think you had it in you."

Oliver fluttered at such unwonted approbation. "Well, I — uh, I found hith lecturth uninterethting."

"That's putting it mildly," agreed Bill. "I hear that you and Goldman and I were the only absentees from the sit-out."

Snead nodded, staring owlishly.

"Who did you go to? Prexy? Or Dean Wittig? I'm anxious to know, for a reason."

"I — " he began to weave back and forth on his chair — "I wath talking to Uncle about it after that club meeting. We went to thee Dean Wittig Thaturday night."

"Anyone else there?"

"No."

"Did the dean mention his niece?"

"No. That ith, I don't think tho." The featherless owl shook his head uncertainly.

"How did he take the news?"

"He *theemed* quite dithturbed. He thaid he would thee to it thoon. But — "

"But what?" persisted Bill.

"Well, my uncle wathn't thatithfied. He went to the chairman of the board."

"Hm. I just wondered. I heard Wittig tell someone after class this morning that Karpen might be back. He said it's possible there was some misunderstanding; that there was doubt as to whether it was Mr. Karpen or one of the students who was at fault. I figured he had this crazy rumor about Sam and communism in his mind. I don't know who started it, but I aim to find out. Okay. Thanks. Get back to the grind."

He rose and left the room. Oliver watched him out with solemn, wise eyes.

Bill marched over to his appointment. As he neared the building he caught sight of Colley Corbett leaving by another door. His swaggering gait was evident even in the shadows.

Colley had avoided Bill after their tangle on Monday evening. He had pretended to be sound asleep when Bill finally discovered him and had deliberately stayed that way until Bill left the next morning for breakfast. He was not anxious to face those piercing dark blue eyes. How he was going to get by with his version of the incident, he didn't know. He merely trusted that he had friends enough to believe it. At least he hoped there would be enough division of opinion so that he would not be bearing all the blame of it. If that happened, he decided he would just come out and put Edda on the spot. After all, she had got him into it and she could take what was coming. But he was fairly sure she would not squeal on him, and in time it would all blow over. Anyway, it was the best story he had been able to invent on the spur of the moment.

Even Colley, however, was amazed at the varied versions he heard throughout the day. He had underestimated Edda's imagination.

Bill was ushered into the board room. The president and several officials sat facing him, on the opposite side of the long, polished table. They were board members, perhaps. Bill didn't know anyone but Dr. Barnett and Dean Wittig.

"We understand," began the president, "that you have some knowledge of the incident that took place on the campus walk Monday evening, and also that you have taken part in certain class meetings called by Mr. Karpen. Will you please tell us what you know?"

Bill complied. He was careful to give in detail the protests that he and Sam had made at the meeting. Then he was cross-examined. It seemed to him that they were trying in every possible way to trip him up and make him contradict what he had already told. The men were grim-visaged and ominous. Altogether it was not a pleasant experience. He wondered what Colley had told them. He wished he could have been the first one to talk.

He met Verna on his way back.

"Don't let them get you down," he warned her.

"I'm scared to death!" she confessed.

"Just tell the truth and stick to it. Leave the rest to the Lord and don't worry."

She cast a forlorn, trembling look up at him.

Actually, the ordeal was not as unfamiliar to Verna as to Bill, for she had been used all her life to harshness and autocratic dealing. But when they became personal in their questions about her attacker, and wormed out of her the origin of her prejudice against Colley, she felt like collapsing.

They requested first that she tell in detail what happened on the campus walk.

While she was describing the incident, one of the younger members interrupted.

"Miss Schiffelgruber, you say that Sam Goldman was your rescuer, not your attacker. May I ask if you — shall we say — admire Sam Goldman?"

Verna blushed to the roots of her amber hair. "Y-yes, of course." She struggled hard not to give herself away by stammering. "Most all the students admire him."

A general grin went the rounds.

"I mean," persisted the interrogator, "do you find him more attractive — to you, that is — than other fellows?"

She hesitated, Bill had told her to stick to the truth.

"I think he is an outstanding young man," she said stoutly and reddened again.

The questioner raised his eyebrows meaningfully at the other men, as if to say, "There you have it; she's defending her lover." He probed further.

"Let me ask one more question. Could you see the face of the man who seized you?"

"N-no. It was too dark. But I know it was Colley."

"How do you know?"

"Because — well, I had — I had —" she could not bring herself to tell of his former advances.

The man gave a supercilious smirk. "I take it you mean you had had some experience before. You knew the feeling of his arms, for instance."

Verna turned crimson. "Yes, I guess you could put

it that way." Her voice was almost a whisper. If they would only stop!

"Perhaps you have cause to dislike Colley Corbett?" Reluctantly she nodded. The others exchanged looks.

"Answer truthfully now. If you had been sure that the man was Sam Goldman, and not Colley Corbett, would you have screamed?" His tone said, "I've got you now!"

"Sam would never have done that!" insisted Verna boldly with fire.

A murmur of amusement ran down the length of the table. The board's glances implied, "That tells you what you *really* wanted to know!"

There were only two men among them who, she felt, were not as antagonistic as the dean and the others. When they had all finished with her, however, she had the feeling that no matter what she had meant to say, she had betrayed Sam and given the wrong impression of him. Her heart was heavy. If she had done Sam any harm after all he had done for her, she would never, never forgive herself.

In hopeless confusion she returned to the dorm and went straight upstairs.

She was still using her own room, for Edda had not yet come back. Her very despair drove her to hunt up her Bible once more. She had not opened it for several weeks. Her book mark was there in the first letter of John where she had been reading long ago. Her heart yearned for help. Never before had she known such depression. She was convinced that all her troubles were her own fault.

"If we confess our sins He is faithful and just to forgive us our sins and to cleanse us. . . ." Those were the only words she saw on the page. She tried to force her eyes to go on, but it seemed as if her gaze was stuck right there. The more she looked, the more conscious she was that she needed to be cleansed. Her willfulness seemed vile, her cheating inexcusable.

She saw her disloyalty that night when she decided to take Edda's way instead of the way of the Lord that she had been taught. Slow tears crept down her cheeks. She slid to her knees.

"Oh Lord, forgive me!" she cried aloud. "I'm an awful sinner. I didn't realize it."

She seized the Book again. It seemed as if there was no hope for her. She had known to do right and had chosen wrong. Where could she go for peace? Her eyes sought the place on the page again . . . "He is faithful and just to forgive . . . and to cleanse." Like a healing flood the words seemed to wash away the terrible guilt on her soul. It never occurred to her to realize that Edda Wittig would have roared with ridicule at the idea of Verna being a terrible sinner. It was God who mattered now, not Edda Wittig.

Eagerly she turned the page back to read the whole chapter. Verse after verse spoke to her heart. "The blood of Jesus Christ . . . cleanseth from all sin . . . If we walk in the light as He is in the light we have fellowship." Fellowship! That was what she had been seeking ever since she came to college. Someone who would always be there and always be friendly. Someone to pal around with. And here God Himself was offering her just that and she had shoved it aside. She had the feeling she could reach out and hold Him now, close to her, and that He would never leave her. She finally rose from her knees. She felt light. None of her outward circumstances had changed, but she was aware that her lips were curling upward in a smile. She hadn't felt like smiling for days — weeks, it seemed.

She ran down to find Mrs. Ross.

But there was no one there. Even Rose and Mrs. Ross had been called upon to testify. She went back to her room to study and wait for them.

Rose was astonished at the information the college officials already had about her family and her relatives in Israel. They asked minute questions about her brother's past, especially what he had been doing the last couple of years. Had he ever been in trouble with the law? Over and over they made her tell why she had started college first, what she knew of his newspaper experiences, and whether she was acquainted with any of his former friends. It was all very bewildering. She could not see what connection it had with the present situation.

It was nearly ten o'clock and she was worn out when it was over. She went back to her room, sank into a chair and covered her face. Her beloved college seemed to have let her down. She longed to be home and out of it all. But then she remembered that it was as if she had no home any more. Was there anything left in the world to depend on? She glanced toward the framed photographs of her parents. Shocked, she jumped up and smothered a scream.

Her mother's picture was on the floor, torn almost in two. The delicate walnut frame was splintered. And on the glass of her father's photograph was the word "JEW" scrawled with lipstick.

She seized his picture and wiped it off carefully, pressing it to her and sobbing. "Oh Lord! When will this end? Why can't they let us alone!"

Tenderly she picked up the torn picture, laid the pieces together and smoothed them out. It seemed as if it was her own heart that had been mangled. She longed to talk to Sam, but the young people had been instructed at their interviews not to try to get in touch with him in any way.

Sam had been promised a discharge from the hospital Wednesday afternoon. He assumed that Bill would come after him. But he waited impatiently and no Bill appeared. His orders were to rest as much as possible; that was difficult.

An early supper was served him which he was too restless to enjoy. When the tray was taken away, a nurse came up to announce that a car was waiting for him.

He was surprised to see the president's own luxurious limousine. He was impressed. No one was in it but the chauffeur.

Sam was glad to rest back on the soft upholstery. He had not realized that he would feel so weak. Even the thought of getting back to concentrated study and make-up assignments made his head ache.

When they arrived at the college, Sam was astonished to find that the chauffeur was driving him to the main administration building instead of to the men's dorm. He was about to question him when Dean Wittig himself came out to meet him.

"Dr. Barnett would like you to come in here first," he explained unceremoniously.

CHAPTER 20

Edda Wittig was in New York City all day without going near the hospital. Toward evening she called her father's nurse.

"Mr. Wittig is out of the oxygen tent," she told her, "and he wants very much to see you."

"Oh, he knows I can't stand hospitals! They make me deathly sick."

"I'm simply giving you his message," replied the nurse in a voice of ice.

"Okay, okay! Tell him I'll try to make it tomorrow."

The nurse said something unintelligible and hung up.

Edda jiggled the instrument. "Hello, hello!" But there was no response. She tried looking daggers at the end of the receiver. It was frustrating. She slammed the thing down. "Is there no peace anywhere?" She went and poured herself a drink. It didn't do any good. She got another. She dreaded unspeakably a trip to the hospital.

That night she called Colley's brother, Lee Corbett. He gladly offered to take her out. She had tried in vain to get Edward Karpen at the old address he had given her. She decided that he must be out of town.

She enjoyed elaborating to Lee on the incident at school in which Colley had played such a prominent part. She knew that Lee was proud of his brother, so she added little details that she thought would please him. Then she described the sit-out; it seemed very funny to her after several cocktails.

"By the way," put in Lee, "that man who was fired — wasn't he the one who came over to our table last week at the 24 Club?

Edda nodded. "That's the one. He's the most. He's terrific."

"I saw him down at our place this morning. He has rented a room over the studio. He's practicing his judo. Does right well, too. I'm surprised. He didn't look to me like the type."

Edda raised her fineline brows. She was thinking fast. It surprised her, too. Why would he be interested, at his age? He must be over forty. But all she said was, "Well, you never know, do you?"

But she pleaded weariness and begged to be taken home early. She soon had Edward Karpen on the phone.

"I'm dying to tell you all about our sit-out!" She talked excitedly. It was not difficult to persuade Mr. Karpen to take her out again, late as it was.

She thought her evening quite thrilling, especially because he took her to an off-beat place that she had never heard of. Every little while he would revert to the doings at college. He milked her of every drop of information. He seemed most interested in everything she could tell him about Sam Goldman. He put so many queries to her that she finally said, with an inscrutable look, "You don't like that guy any more than I do, do you?"

He raised his brows as if he was not ready to commit himself, and smoothed his tiny mustache, once to the left, once to the right.

"I'm interested in the communistic character you managed to assign to him. You recognize, of course, that he is anything but that. He is quite blind to the values of communism. He is loyal to the bone to what he calls freedom and liberty." There was an open sneer in his tone.

Edda put on a Mona Lisa smile. "How stupid do you think I am?"

He laughed at that and showed his beautiful set of white teeth.

"Actually, I think you are smart, very, very smart." He leaned closer and lowered his voice. "Edda, I've been watching you for a long time. I believe that you and I see things pretty much eye to eye. I wonder if you wouldn't like to work with me."

If he expected her to light up and snatch at the bait, he was mistaken. She narrowed her eyes and smiled. "It might be pleasant," she countered. "Tell me more." She smiled archly.

They talked for two hours. When Karpen left, Edda's gray green eyes had a new glint in them.

By Wednesday noon she was on her way back to college. The hospital called again and again, but there was no answer.

On the plane Edda picked up a newspaper. Glancing idly through it she noted that there was a fresh flare-up of trouble between the Arabs and Israel. She fairly licked her lips. In a very small way she now felt that she herself had a part in that conflict. She intended that that part should not remain small.

She directed the airport limousine to her uncle's house rather than the dorm. Karpen had promised to phone and prepare him for her visit. He greeted her without warmth. He was not at all sure that he was pleased to have her an initiate. But he could not help admiring the keen grasp she had of all his various involvements. He really wished that she didn't know so much about him. Karpen, he felt, had taken undue advantage of his absence and of the fact that the girl was his niece. But Karpen was his superior and his it was to do or die.

He discussed the board meeting freely.

"I will be as glad as you to relieve the college of the presence of Goldman and Lodge," he told her. "I believe if one goes the other will. They hinder the progress of the student body as a whole. Lodge's religious propaganda is actually a power to be feared. But our greatest opponents in the meeting tonight with Goldman are going to be our friends Ebenezer Snead and Barnett himself. They are a couple of old sticks-in-the-mud. Not a progressive thought in their makeup. I might handle Snead, but it's a tough thing to buck the president in a board meeting, unless I'm sure of a heavy majority."

Edda narrowed her green eyes and thought a minute. "Why not dispose of the president?"

Her uncle looked startled.

"*Dispose* of him?" He shook his head.

She gave a careless laugh. "I don't mean what you think I mean. But just put him out of the running for a few hours. If you'll invite him over to dinner this evening to discuss the student situation, I'll see to it that he doesn't come to the meeting."

"Now, Edda!" Dean Wittig was thoroughly alarmed. He had seen his niece operate before; he knew she was utterly uninhibited by principles of moral conduct. "Look here, girl. I'm the dean here. I am not anxious to end up behind bars or have a scandal connected with my name."

She chortled gaily. "Don't you give it a thought, Uncle Raymond. You will know nothing about it. This

202

is my little project, and I give you my word it will not taint your fair name. Now, I'll see to the table and all, but it's up to you to have the dinner sent up from the restaurant. I'm not going to cook. But I will—ah—*edit* the food. I am going to disappear before he gets here. Now go ahead and call him."

So it was that when Sam, returning from the hospital, followed the dean into the sacrosanct board room the first thing the dean did after calling the meeting to order was to explain that unfortunately the president had been taken ill a short time ago and would not be able to be there. Dr. Barnett had asked that the dean take charge.

Most of the board members were present. On one side of the long rectangular table sat Ebenezer Snead, looking more than usually grim. Ranged with him were three elderly men, a judge, a banker, and a publisher, all of whom had been with the college since its founding. Along the other side of the table, lined up vis-a-vis like knights armed for a joust, were four younger men, all fresh from educational mills; two writers, a doctor of psychology, and a bright, plump clergyman.

Dean Wittig officiated at the head of the board. Sam, utterly mystified, was placed at the foot.

The dean cleared his throat and hesitated; he was undertaking a most unpleasant task.

Dean Wittig looked straight at Sam. "Young man, you are aware, no doubt, of the twofold accusation that has been brought against your communistic activity and personal assault on a female classmate. Both are serious. What have you to say for yourself?"

Sam stared from one to another, chagrined and thoroughly angry.

If he only felt better he could think more clearly.

He rose to his feet struggling for self-control.

"Gentlemen," he shook his head, "you are mistaken in your man. This is absurd. I am not the one you want."

"Sit down, Samuel Goldman," commanded the dean sternly. "It has been reported to me that you have been openly attacking and belittling the constitution of the United States. And you have also showed a debased nature in that you attacked a fellow class member, a girl, Verna Mae Schiffelgruber, after dark, right on the campus."

"*I* attacked her!" ejaculated Sam. "Oh no. Your story is all twisted, sir. She was attacked all right, and I heard her scream. When I tried to free her, Col—her attacker turned on me and beat me up. As for that other charge, that's ludicrous. We were indignant at what we considered Prof. Karpen's communistic influence and my friend and I spoke up, that's all." Sam was puffing with weakness; talking was still a painful process.

The young psychologist expert put in a word.

"I would like to have the young lady—" he consulted his notes—"Edda Wittig, recalled, please."

Edda was brought in. She did not glance toward Sam.

"Please repeat for us, in his presence, Miss Wittig, what you have recorded of this young man's statements."

Edda read from Tracy's notes.

"I think an apt suggestion would be whether or not to amend the basic fundamentals of the constitution of the United States."

Sam listened in horror.

"Oh, but sirs—"

"Just a minute, Mr. Goldman. Now please tell us, Miss Wittig, what you saw from the window of the classroom."

"I saw my roommate walking past the building where we were toward the dormitory. She met this man and a friend of his. They talked for some minutes. After the fellows passed out of sight she continued on. Then all of a sudden a figure appeared out of the dark and seized her. I heard her start to scream. Immediately I sent one of our group, Colley Corbett, to help her. I saw him grab this person and knock him down; he hit him pretty hard, I guess. He's very strong. You can see the result."

Edda gave a mocking jerk of her head toward Sam's battered face.

Stunned at her audacity, Sam glared back at her, trying to make her flinch. But she held her cool poise and stared him down with composure.

It looked like a clear case against Sam.

"But sir," he addressed the dean, "she is mistaken. It was just the other way around!"

"It is your word against hers," returned the dean coldly.

"But I have witnesses—the girl herself, Verna, who was attacked."

"She has admitted that she did not see her attacker."

"My roommate, Bill Lodge, was there!"

"He, too, has testified that he did not actually witness the attack. When he arrived you and Mr. Corbett were struggling on the ground. You and Mr. Lodge would naturally stick together in your stories. You are close friends. So you see, Mr. Goldman, there are two witnesses against you, and only you to speak for yourself. It is a very unfortunate situation." He gave an impression of spitting out unpalatable food.

"But, gentlemen," began Sam once more.

The dean raised his hand to stop him. "We shall investigate further, Mr. Goldman. But you do admit that you were there at that place at that time Monday evening?"

"Yes, but—"

"And you do admit that the statement read from the records was made by you?"

"Yes, but Dean Wittig, I was being sarcastic. I didn't mean it."

"A very weak argument, young man. It is rather late

205

to decide that you didn't mean it. If you wish now to retract it well and good. But this college must take its stand."

"You can ask the rest of the class," cried Sam. "They know I was sarcastic because I hated the stuff Mr. Karpen was handing us."

"We have examined several of the class members. We have not found that to be the case. I'm sorry. In fact, I am disappointed in you."

Sam's black eyes flashed fire.

"Well, I must say I am disappointed in you, Dean Wittig, and in this college. This is an egregious misrepresentation of facts. If you all want to take a stand against communism," he blazed, looking around the table from one to another, "I suggest that you look into the dean's own background and find out why he practically promised a student only yesterday morning that Mr. Karpen would be back here!"

Dean Wittig merely raised his eyebrows with a cool shrug. "That will do, young man. Your insinuations will accomplish nothing. You will be informed of the final decision very soon. Until then, you may be permitted to remain, but do not leave the grounds. The penalty for the double misdemeanor will probably be suspension or even expulsion."

Sam staggered back the quarter of a mile to his dormitory.

CHAPTER 21

Rose was reading a letter from her mother when Bill called her on the phone.

". . . and so for this last time, Rosie, I am begging you, please give up this incredible *meshumed* infatuation. You see what is happening in Israel—constant border trouble there, and riots in Jerusalem. And now the mosque on Mt. Zion has been bombed. As it is a masterpiece of art, this will cause a furor. The Arabs are accusing Jewish agitators, but of course it was done by fanatics. All this is because of the sin of our people. God is visiting judgment on us because our children are departing from Jehovah."

There was more. The letter was long and blurred with tears. Her poor mother's last weapon now was to blame on Rose all the sorrows of Israel. But Rose still loved her mother. She had been in the bonds of blindness so recently herself that she understood.

She longed to talk to Sam.

Her buzzer sounded. Perhaps Mrs. Ross needed her.

"Call for you, Rosie," smiled the girl in charge at the desk. "Sounds like your big blond!"

"Yes?" lilted Rose.

"Rose, Sam is back." Bill's voice sounded dark with fury. Rose waited. "Rose, they have put him through the third degree in the board room and he is done up. They even let him walk back to the dorm."

Rose made a little sound of indignation.

"That's not all, Rose." Bill was struggling to swallow something in his throat. "It looks as if they're going to blame everything on him!"

"Oh Bill!" wailed Rose. "They can't *do* that!"

"They're doing it, Rose. When I was in there it

looked to me as if the cards were stacked against him. That's nothing but anti-Semitism. I'm convinced of it."

"Wh-what are they going to do to Sam?"

"I don't know yet. Sam thinks the board is divided. Prexy was sick. Dean Wittig presided. I don't trust that guy for some reason. Too much like his niece. But they have threatened suspension. They may even expel him. If they do, I leave, too. And there will be others."

Rose had nothing to say. Slow tears coursed down her cheeks.

"Rose. You there?"

"Yes, Bill, yes. Oh, Bill, it seems as if everything is going to pieces!"

"I guess it is, dear." He paused a moment. "We'll have to remember that when that begins, we're to look up and rejoice. That's a pretty large order. Too much for us."

"I know what you're going to say," she put in gently. "That *He* can do it. Didn't you say that He is the God of the Impossible?"

"Oh, Rose! Yes! Forgive me for cryin' on your shoulder!"

She gave a low laugh. "Good night—dear. Give Sam my love, and tell him I'll be praying.

Bill had to rub his sleeve across his eyes before he turned from the phone. What a girl.

By this time letters were coming into the local paper giving the citizens' view of the whole case. It had had considerable publicity. Anti-Semitic feeling was popping up here and there. Editorials discussed the problem. By the end of the week letters to the editor had appeared in the local paper from individuals, even as far as the New York area. "I live in New York now," wrote one, "but I used to be in college there. I think it is getting to be too much when a girl can't walk back to the dorm on an evening on her own campus without being attacked—and by another student, too. If all the

Jews were sent back to their precious Israel and bombed it would be the best thing that ever happened to this country."

Edda had been looking through the Letters to the Editor section for several days. When she found that one she smiled complacently. It was signed Edwina Whitmore. If anyone searched thoroughly, Edwina's picture could be found in the college yearbook of fifteen years back. It had pleased Edda to find names that resembled her own. She loved to live dangerously.

All the students were reading the newspapers more than usual these days; war seemed more imminent than ever. Soviet Russia was determined to wipe out Israel. All commentators agreed that as soon as a real move was made in that direction it would mean total war.

The college authorities were deep in plans for building enough underground shelters to take care of all of its students. Columnists hinted strongly that congressmen, senators, and even Security Council members were resorting to advice from fortune tellers and spiritist mediums. No one knew whether to believe it or not. The very rumor made the foundations of government seem to totter.

There was more talk than ever of nations, and business firms, and even churches getting together in mergers of one kind or another, yet never were they so bitterly divided—the churches, worst of all.

The top brass of nations as well as of corporations were frantically scrambling about, sitting up nights, calling emergency conferences to find a way to salvage what they had always thought they possessed.

There were weird reports of voices heard, warning of what was coming. No one knew where they originated. Most people believed them to be broadcast from space stations. But governments denied any knowledge of them.

Here and there came stories of strangers appearing,

warning, and vanishing. Were they true? Or were they the result of overtense nerves?

Deaths from heart failure mounted. Suicides were common. TV horror films did not ease the conditions.

Astronauts brought disturbing reports of meeting strange objects in space. Terror was gaining ground.

Then came news of serious drought in Egypt. Everything was drying up. Plans were being pushed to change the course of smaller rivers. Israel's Jordan was eyed.

In Dean Wittig's political science class the students swamped him with questions he couldn't answer. Bill Lodge was annoyingly ready with authoritative answers from the Bible that infuriated Dean Wittig. Everyone everywhere was suddenly faced with the conditions that had been coming on for some time. It seemed as if they were breaking overnight.

Sam's fate still hung in the balance. Until the five-five board stalemate could be settled, he was permitted to remain on campus and to attend classes. But he was reminded that he was under strict surveillance. That was almost worse than expulsion. Sam was avoided or greeted with silent contempt on campus. Bill took his share of ostracism because he was Sam's friend. Rose was mildly tolerated.

It was galling. The board was too busy with other affairs to take time to come to a decision, although the grapevine had it now that the delay was due to a near split over the struggle for power.

Colley Corbett received a draft notice and departed. All those physically fit, with a lower than C average, were being called. Before he left, Bill had a talk with him.

"Say, Corbett," he said grimly, "you know the truth about that Sam and Verna deal. Why don't you stand up like a man and say you lied?"

"Look, good buddy," Colley sneered, "people don't often get away with calling Colley a liar. You better take it easy. Anyway, how can I do anything? You were there yourself and you couldn't. Gossip never can be straightened out."

"But I've heard you stand by and let kids say things you know aren't true."

"So what?" Colley shrugged. "I'm not a do-gooder. I'll leave that to you, reverend." He gave an ugly chortle.

Bill studied him. Suddenly the other's need rose up before him, urgent and terrifying. He spoke more calmly.

"Corbett," he said, "now you mention it, I've often wondered how you stand with the Lord. Are you fixin' to go to heaven? Or hell? Okay, you can laugh if you want," as Colley guffawed, "but it's *your* life you may be losing, you know."

Colley walked over to him, straightening up and pulling in his abdomen. Bill was not sure but that he was going to hit him. Bill didn't stir.

Instead, Colley clapped a hand on Bill's shoulder and said carelessly, "Cool it, good buddy. I'm satisfied the way I am. If there's a heaven, fine. I'll buy that. But," he spread his hands helplessly, "if not, well, there's nothing I can do about it. I've had my fun!" He flung back a laugh and departed.

A few days before Christmas vacation, Verna received another letter from home, the first since her mother's appeal a month before.

Verna had formed the habit lately of taking her problems to the Lord. She was sleeping in her own room nights, but the rest of the time, she and Edda saw nothing of each other. Verna usually arose very early and, with her Bible, climbed to the big rock behind the dorm and read and prayed.

She was almost afraid to open the letter until she could be alone. She waited until she reached the old stone bench.

It was from the youngest of her brothers, the only

211

one who had made an effort to stand by her. Their father, he said, ordered her to return home at Christmas time. Verna, knowing her father, read between the lines his intention to keep her at home, if she once got back. She had no idea of giving up her education now, even though she had been so disillusioned by the college.

She had refrained from writing all this time, but she knew that now it was time to respond. Yet what was she to say? She opened her Bible. In her regular reading she had come to the twenty-third chapter of Luke. She read it thoughtfully. When she came to "Father, forgive them, for they know not what they do," tears blurred her eyes. She took a sheet of notebook paper and wrote rapidly.

Dear Hen:

Thanks for your letter. I miss you all. I was very bitter for a while about the folks not letting me know about Rich. But I know now that I was just as wrong as they were. Hen, I have learned to know Jesus Christ in a way I never did before. All I used to have was my parents' religion. You know as well as I do that for me it was just "Don't do this" and "Don't do that." I have met some Christian young people here, and I have found that the Lord is not like that. He isn't interested in Do's and Don'ts; He simply wants to come into a heart and live. I love Him now, Hen, and I'm glad.

Tell Father I'm not coming home yet. I'm going to work and earn enough to finish college. Give mother and the rest my love.

The same evening a long distance call came for Edda. She was not to be found. A check revealed that she had not been in her classes all day. The call was repeated an hour later. She was still absent. After the third attempt, the operator asked for Edda's roommate.

Verna went to the phone.

It was George Wittig's nurse. He was still in the

hospital and no better. Edda had never been near him.

"Are you the girl who visited his daughter at Thanksgiving?"

"Yes," admitted Verna, "but I scarcely saw Mr. Wittig."

"I know that. He told me about it. Miss, he is not going to last long. The doctor says that his heart can take another twenty-four hours at most. Mr. Wittig seems desperate to see you. He was set back terribly by having his daughter completely disregard him. He will pay your expenses both ways if you will come. What may I tell him?"

Verna hesitated as long as she dared. The thought of the trip alone and a visit to an almost utter stranger terrified her. Yet he was going to die. She couldn't say no.

"All right," she agreed in a small voice. "Tell him I'll come."

She turned away feeling like a child about to attempt a space flight.

George Wittig knew that his end was near. He was quite aware that his only brother thought him not worth visiting. He didn't blame him. He felt the same way about Raymond. He tried to excuse his daughter's unfilial actions by remembering that she hated hospitals. Nevertheless he was afraid to be alone. His nurses were efficient, good, and kind. They knew how to prepare an oxygen tent or a hypodermic; they could prepare a patient for surgery. But neither of them seemed to have had any training in preparing a patient for the next world. When they became aware of his concern, they sent for a clergyman. Father Morgan was good and kind and efficient, too. He performed his ceremonies just as the nurses performed theirs, only his were supposed to ensure the safety of the soul. But George's soul was not safe yet and he knew it; there were too many long hidden sins that had risen up to plague him. What was to be done about them? It was too late now to try to make up for them. Some were heinous.

Father Morgan had suggested that he confess them, which he did. But just telling a person about them wasn't enough; he still had no peace of mind. He ran through the list of all his acquaintances. Not one, so far as he knew, had real peace of mind, or had ever given any evidence of any assurance of how to get it, except one girl, Edda's roommate, a strange little serious-minded screwball, he had thought her then. She was the only one in all his life who had ever mentioned the name of the Lord with any confidence. He didn't even know her name. But she was the one he turned to.

On the way down the long white hospital corridor Verna prayed as she had never prayed before. It was the first time she had ever been in a hospital. Its immaculate, efficient way of dealing with disease and death rather overpowered her. She had never been sick in her life. This place existed on illnesses. They were its business, just as dry goods was the business of a store, and cattle the business, of a rancher. She felt as helpless to try to deal with the ills of this man she was going to meet as she would feel trying to rope a steer on a Texas cattle ranch, perhaps more so.

She paused outside the door. The nurse was expecting her and ushered her in.

She was shocked at the gray look on Mr. Wittig's face. He looked twenty-years older than he had in his apartment that night. She tried to smile, but she didn't make it.

His hungry eyes drew her to the bedside.

"You came!" His voice was weak. "I wouldn't let them give me any more shots till you got here." He stopped and panted, his eyes drooping shut from weakness.

"That night," he gasped, "you said something about —about—what comes next. You seemed to know what you were talking about." He didn't take his gaze from

214

her. "If you did, tell me now. I'm an awful sinner. Tomorrow will be too late."

Verna's own heart had been hammering till she thought he would hear it. Now all at once she forgot it. She forgot she was just a little country Dutch girl alone in New York City, talking to a stranger. She saw a soul about to take the great step from Today into Tomorrow. She smiled confidently.

She didn't know that the nurse was watching her with keen appraising eyes.

"Yes, I do know, sir," she said. She took from her coat pocket the little New Testament that she had tucked there to read on the plane.

"I'll read it to you, so you will know it's God's own Word and you can trust it. Listen carefully. These words helped me a lot once. 'The blood of Jesus Christ His Son cleanseth us from all sin.' "

His eyes opened wider, as if startled. "Read it again!" he mumbled.

She read it again.

"Blood? Cleanseth?"

"Yes," said Verna with calm eagerness. "He died for us, you know, for all of us. He hadn't sinned, but He took all our sins and died in our place. That's how we can be clean."

"He did that?"

"Yes."

"For me, too?"

"Yes."

"Oh, why did no one ever tell me that?" In his delight he tried to raise his head. "Thank God!" He fell back on the pillow and his life on earth was over. A look of utmost peace settled on the pale features. The nurse seized his wrist, but there was no pulse. She looked up at Verna and shook her head gently.

On the plane on her way back Verna was amazed at the joy in her own heart that she had been chosen to show the way across the great gulf to another soul.

"I never saw death before," she told Sam the next day. They had fallen into the habit of walking up to their rock every day after lunch. Sam was practically isolated from all but a few students who still believed in him. He had found relief in Verna's steady trust and companionship.

"I never realized before what a very short step it is from life to death—well, you could say from death to life, too. For he certainly came out of spiritual death into eternal life just before he left." Verna had forgotten she was talking to one who had been brought up to despise the name of Jesus Christ. "It was the most remarkable experience I ever had. And how I dreaded to go! I'm ashamed of myself. Just think what I would have missed."

Sam studied her, chewing away on his pine needle. There was a tender light in his eyes.

"You know you're quite a gal, VeeEm." He spoke in a more serious tone than usual. Most of his remarks, especially if they verged on the personal, were generally given in a whimsical, teasing way.

She turned quickly and caught his look. Her amber eyes widened an instant and then she glanced away while the pink stole up to her temples. Her old shyness came back upon her suddenly and she jumped up.

"I guess I'd better get back and get to work on that English theme." She didn't quite dare to look at him again.

He chuckled gently and rose, too. But he helped her carefully down the jagged stone stairs instead of letting her make her own way as he usually did.

"I wonder if Edda is back yet. Where on earth do you suppose she is?"

"Who cares? The place is better off without her. I'm glad you quit trying to be like her."

Verna grinned at him, a little sheepishly. "I pulled a lot of 'goo-goos' when I first came, didn't I?" she asked.

He looked puzzled. "A lot of *what?*"

She clapped her hand over her mouth. "Oh! I mean 'boo-boos.' I always get it mixed up. I'll never learn slang."

Sam roared. Then he glanced at her out of the corner of his eye to see if she was hurt. But this time she laughed with him.

"I goofed, didn't I?" she added impishly.

He put an arm around her and gave her a little hug. "VeeEm, you're the most!"

She hummed a little snatch of a song as she went into the dorm. It seemed as if life was almost ready to be pleasant again.

But Mrs. Ross met her at the door, distress on her face. "Do you know where Sam is?"

"I just left him. I'll catch him."

She flew down the steps and ran after him. Bill had just met him and they returned together.

"Your sister has had a letter from home. She has been trying to find you."

They went in to Mrs. Ross' little sitting room. Sam stepped aside to let Verna in too. Since the shadow had been hanging over them the four young people had drawn closer together.

Rose had been crying. She brightened at sight of Sam and handed the letter. It was from Yehudi. He scanned it quickly. What now?

"Read it aloud, the part about Israel," said Rose.

" '. . . and now that the Mosque has been bombed the Arabs have accepted the price Ben Gurion offered.' "

"They destroy it and then demand the money for it?" cried Bill indignantly.

Sam looked up. "Well what would you expect?"

"But that's not all. Read on," urged Rose tensely.

" 'Everybody expects war anyway. We pay for Mt. Moriah and then they will fight us to steal it back. Our people have swarmed into the old city since the money was paid. The Arabs have seized all the boys and girls who cross over. They plan to *sell them* before the war

217

starts, to get all the money they can. It may be the only way the children can escape war, but we would rather see them die than that. Our David is among those who have been seized!' "

Verna saw Sam's face grow gray. "I remember when Davey was born. He's only 15." He choked and swallowed hard before he could go on. " 'We believe he is still alive but we watch the slave markets every day to catch a glimpse of him. The worst of it is that we Jews may not buy back our own children. They are sold to foreigners. My father is still alive but very sick. We are afraid his mind will go. Oh, can't you find someone over there who would come and bid on the auction block for David? But if you do it must not be known that we have anything to do with it. It must all be done secretly . . .' "

There was more. The agony of the older brother was bleeding through the pages. He described some of the horrors the children endured. Sam went to the window to hide his face from the others.

"I will go, of course," he said huskily.

"No, Sam," objected Rose. "It would do no good. You would be known instantly for a Jew. It must be an American. But the price would be out of sight. They know the Americans do not use slaves, but they know Americans are rich and kind and will pay high prices to get children out. Money is what the enemy wants just now."

"I think this is where I come in," spoke up Bill.

They all turned to him, startled.

"You! Oh, Bill! It would be terribly dangerous. We couldn't ask you to do that!"

"You didn't," grinned Bill. "David will soon be *my* little cousin." He looked straight across at Rose for confirmation. Her eyes held his and adored him. She stood up, very straight and tall, and in her dignified way—"like an empress" Bill always said—she walked over and took her place beside him. His arm went around her.

"Yes," she smiled solemnly, "of course Bill will go and get *our* cousin David."

Verna looked wonderingly from one to another. It seemed to her that more strange and terrible things had happened in the last few weeks than she had ever heard of before in anyone's lifetime.

"I will start as soon as I can arrange it," Bill announced. Rose looked up at him with utmost confidence. "Yes," she said significantly. "Tomorrow may be too late."

"I want to go with you, Bill. Two are better than one."

"Not this time, old man. I'll manage better alone. Stay and take care of Rose for me. Ask the Lord's blessing on us, Mother Ross."

They gathered around her; quietly and lovingly she committed Bill and Rose, the boy David, and the whole of tortured Israel into the hands of the "God of the Impossible."

CHAPTER 22

Bill spent hours closeted with representatives of Jewish agencies in New York City. It was while he was there that he discovered that Edda Wittig had disappeared from the country with Edward Karpen. "Good riddance," he wrote to Rose.

The hours seemed endless, in view of the frightful plight of the Israeli children. Even if Bill was successful, he could save only one of hundreds. Uprisings in the Moslem world continued. Reports of bitter anti-Semitism had grown to terrifying proportions, even in the United States. At last he was told that his passage would soon be cleared.

Rose had heard no more from her parents. It seemed that her mother's threat in her last plea was going to be carried out. But Rose made it a practice to write home regularly. In every letter she set forth something of what Bill and Mrs. Ross had been teaching her. She saw to it that each one contained some item of fulfilled prophecy; then she would present again the claims of Jesus Christ and reiterate her love for her father and mother.

"They have cast me off anyway," she said to Mrs. Ross sadly one day, "so I don't see how it can make things any worse. And I believe they still love me enough so that they will read the letters."

When the news of David's danger came, she reminded them to read the third chapter of Joel. "The nations *are* gathering," she wrote. "Egypt will be punished. But all these things are taking place 'that it might be fulfilled which was written by the prophet.' Even unbelievers know that the day of the Lord is near. It is the blood alone that cleanses. Moses taught us that. The blood of Jesus Christ God's Son; nothing else. Oh, believe Him now. Tomorrow may be too late!"

They had written very little to their parents about Sam's dilemma. Time enough for that if he really was expelled.

After Bill returned from New York, he and Sam stayed close to their room waiting for a call to confirm Bill's flight. Oliver Snead was there sitting at his desk, hunched over a photography magazine. The phone in the corridor rang; Bill jumped to get it. But the call was from the main office for Sam.

"Mr. Goldman, this is Dean Wittig's secretary." The voice seemed to come from a deep freeze. "The college board is in session and you are to come to the office immediately."

Sam set his lips. Somberly he poked his head in at the bedroom door.

"This is *it!*" He tossed them a wave of his hand and left.

Bill sat slumped, his head in his hands, praying silently.

All at once he realized that Oliver Snead was at his elbow. He had some snapshots in his hand. Bill shoved him aside. "Not now," he said gruffly, "take 'em away."

"But I think they might be of thome help to Tham," chirped Oliver.

Bill didn't half listen. No one ever listened to Oliver Snead.

"I took a lot of thnapth that night it happened," he explained, undaunted. "I was exthperimenting with infra-red. Tham might need thethe." He thrust them rudely under Bill's nose.

Bill started to push him away again. Then he sat up and fairly choked the poor little fellow.

"What did you say? Pictures? What are they?" He seized them. They were a series of ten snaps showing Verna talking to Bill and Sam, Verna alone, and then Colley approaching, seizing her, and Sam's sudden rescue. There was even one of Bill tossing Colley through the air.

"Snead! You old goat! Why didn't you turn up with these before?" Bill fairly screamed at him.

Oliver shrugged his tiny shoulder. "I didn't get them back until a couple of dayth ago. I didn't know whether Tham would need them or not."

But Bill was already long gone and didn't hear his explanation. He tore up the stairs of the administration building three at a time and burst without ceremony into the board room.

He stalked straight up to the astonished president.

"Sir, I apologize for breaking in like this." His voice was stentorian. If any one of them had been

221

talking he wouldn't have been heard. "I don't know what you have been saying to Sam. But I have final conclusive proof here of his innocence, in these pictures." He explained their source. He didn't know Ebenezer Snead, so he didn't catch his beaming look of pride and amazement. All he saw was the relief and gratitude in Sam's face.

"Dr. Barnett," he continued as the pictures were being passed from hand to hand, "I think it is now in order for me to demand two things: a public apology before the student body and in the newspapers; also, a further investigation of certain people who have been attempting to bring communism and anti-Semitism into this school. I refer to Mr. Karpen, Dean Wittig and his niece. If I am wrong, I am sorry. But I feel that they deserve something of what they have been handing out to my friends. They have a fine line of talk about civil rights and equality for all. I think it is time they began to practice some of it." He gathered up his snapshots. "Come on, Sam."

Dean Wittig's face was a study in red.

Bill was not careful to close the door too gently on the buzz of comment in the room.

Neither of the boys could speak for a few moments. They stopped on the walk and beamed at each other.

"Didn't I tell you the Lord would work it out?" Bill exulted. "Oh, that Snead character! Can anyone ever explain why he didn't bring those bits of paper out before?"

They both broke down and laughed hysterically.

"And here we thought he was such an odd ball, always fiddling with his cameras."

"He is an odd ball," insisted Bill. "But he'll probably turn out to be a genius of some kind. You never know."

Their steps took them automatically to Holley Hall. They rushed in to the desk where Rose held sway.

"Call Mother Ross, and VeeEm, quick!" cried Sam, beaming.

Rose looked frantically from one to the other.

"Don't tell me something good has happened, at last?" she cried unbelievingly when she saw their smiles.

They gathered in Mrs. Ross' sitting room. When all the details of the story had been recited several times and rejoiced over, Sam suddenly thought of Oliver.

"Let's go and thank the old unfeathered two-legged thing!" He winked at Verna.

"Yes, we must get back. I don't want to miss the call from the airport."

The shadow of Bill's approaching trip blanketed them again, but somehow the fact that their prayers had been answered in Sam's case gave strength to their faith for Bill and young David.

Rose's yearning eyes followed Bill out.

She heaved a deep sigh after they had gone.

"Things happen so fast these days that you scarcely can get your breath," said Rose. "It's like the roller coaster at Coney Island!" There was a bit of a catch in her laugh. She was all too aware that it was possible she might never see Bill again on earth.

Early the next morning Sam phoned to say that he had taken Bill to the plane at 3 A.M.

"I didn't call you. I thought you'd had enough disturbance. Besides, we have been warned to keep this all as quiet as possible."

Rose went about with her heart in the skies all day. Every thought was a prayer for Bill.

Sam had offered to contact friends of theirs to get money for Bill to use for the payment he would have to make. But Bill refused it.

"Thank God I have it myself," responded Bill fervently. "Remember, it's *my* young cousin too, Sam old boy." Bill laid a brotherly hand on his shoulder.

Sam studied him. "Bill," he said soberly, "I'm not one to make speeches. But I've puzzled over what I've ever done to deserve a friend like you."

They were waiting at the airport. Bill laughed light-heartedly. "Don't forget there's a lot to be said on the other side, too. After all, what has any one of us ever done to deserve all that God has given us, Sam? It's all grace. It had to be. I only wish — " Bill paused.

"Yeah, I know what you're going to say. You wish I were — like you are. I mean, a Christian." Sam was serious. "I guess maybe," he hesitated, "you won't have to worry about that any longer."

Bill's eyes filled. "You mean that, Sam, old boy?"

Sam grinned. "I tried my best, Bill, to be like you. I did all the things I knew to do and it didn't work. So I just gave up and did nothing. And one morning not long ago, I guess it was yesterday — it seems ages — I woke up and I knew I belonged to Him." He opened his hands in a characteristic shrug. "I didn't do anything about it. I just knew."

"Sam, that's the best news I've had since Rose said yes!" He gripped his friend's hand till Sam winced. "Well, here comes the plane. Pray for us."

That was the last morning of classes before the holidays. After lunch, when most of the students had gone their ways, Sam hunted up Rose. Neither of them had mentioned going home for Christmas. They were both aware of the complexity of the situation. They knew their parents and Jewish tradition well enough to be certain that once a definite stand had been taken, nothing would change it.

"You staying here for Christmas?" asked Sam.

Rose drooped a little. "I — guess so. Mrs. Ross said I might. I'll be all right, Sam. You go on home. Write and let me know how they are. Bill ought to be back before the holidays are over." She sighed.

Sam shook his head slowly. "I don't think I'd be any more welcome than you, now, Rosie." He waited for her reaction.

She glanced up from her desk work. A slow light

like sunrise began to glow in her face. "Oh, Sam! You know Him, too!" She flung her arms around her brother, glad that there was no one around; Sam would have hated that. He grinned.

"Yes. It was like being blind before, wasn't it?"

"That's just the way I felt. A person really doesn't know what it is to see if he's always been blind. Oh, Sam! Do you suppose the folks will ever, ever see?"

"I kind of think so, Rose. I believe we can ask the Lord to do that. After all, when I think of how He solved my problem with those pictures! He knew it all the time. It must be that way with everything. He has the answers. It's just that we don't know them yet. And He won't let us look in the back of the book for them. It probably wouldn't be good for us. Well, I think I'll just stay, too. I arranged with the building and grounds superintendent to let me work. Otherwise I'd have to get out." They walked together to the door.

They were both remembering past holidays. Their homecomings had always been so bright.

"But I wouldn't change it," said Rose softly. "It's hard, but it's worth it, isn't it?"

He nodded. He was watching a car that drew up and parked at the entrance curb.

"Rosie!" he cried. "Do you see what I see?"

He raced down the walk. A familiar figure was stepping out of the car. "Papa!" He fairly screamed with joy. Rose was already clasped in her mother's arms.

"We thought it would be nice to drive you home," smiled Mr. Goldman. "Then we could talk longer." He beamed. "We have a lot to talk about — now, Mama and I."

Rose and her mother were laughing and crying. Without being told, they knew that some change had taken place. Time enough to talk it all out on the way home.

"I'll run up and pack my bag," Rose said. "Come in while I get it, Mama. I won't be but a few minutes."

They left their parents in the big comfortable lounge in Holley Hall and hurried off.

While Rose was joyously throwing a few things into her suitcase she suddenly remembered Verna. She stopped. Things had been happening so fast that it hadn't occurred to her to ask Verna where she was going to spend the holidays. She hurried out to her mother.

"May I bring a girl with me, if she can come?" she asked.

"When did you ever have to ask, my Rosie?" Her mother's face was wreathed in smiles. Gone was the harried look of distress.

Rose flew up to Verna's room. "You're to come home with me, honey. Now!" She hugged her. "Oh, the Lord is so good to us. Hurry, VeeEm. I'll see you downstairs."

A word to Mrs. Ross and a warm hug.

"Praise the Lord, darling! He *is* faithful!"

"Oh, Mother Ross, you will pray for Bill?"

"Of course, child. He'll be back. Shall I send him right on if he comes here?"

"Just guess!" laughed Rose.

Off in the crisp winter sunshine they rode. Verna's heart was in a whirl. This was what she had passed up before, for what? *How foolish can you be?* she thought to herself. *But how did I know?* She stole a glance at the back of Sam's head. He was driving for his father. She could see how proud his parents were of him. And they gave Verna the cordial welcome that had always been so ready for every friend their children invited home.

They stopped at a pleasant wayside coffee shop for supper and crowded into a booth.

"You can sit between Mama and Papa, Rosie," suggested Sam. "You're the baby." He grinned.

Verna wondered whether Sam really made an effort to sit beside her or whether that was only her own wishful thinking. But she caught him looking at her more than once in a way that brought the pink up in her cheeks and sent a thrill through her that was beyond any joy she had ever known. And when the others had finished and were sliding out he looked down at her again and held her hand close in his. "Shalom, VeeEm!" he whispered, and her heart leaped up in her eyes.

Dark had settled down when they started on.

"Wouldn't you like me to drive awhile, Sam?" his father offered.

"No, you sit back with Rosie and Mama. I'm all right. It's not far now. We'll be home in an hour."

Verna felt a new fluttering. *He does care!* she told herself. It was hard to believe. Soon his hand reached over and sought hers. She turned and he smiled. Oh, how different from Colley's caresses. *What a fool I was!*

Rose snuggled down between her father and mother. "Now tell me about it," she said.

They knew what she meant.

"Well," began her father, "it was Mama first who insisted that we get a Bible and hunt up all the places you told us about."

"Yes," put in her mother, "but it was Papa who understood it first."

"That's because I had a very good rabbi to teach me when I was young, Mama."

"But what made you see?" persisted Rose. "We were all so blind!"

"It was just yesterday," explained Mama Goldman. "When your letter came telling us the wonderful thing that your Bill is doing. We couldn't believe it. We knew that it wasn't just to be kind to you. It was too big a thing for a Gentile to do unless he loved all our people. And all at once I saw how God's

227

Son loved us to do what He did. Oh, Rosie, how I cried when I heard about those poor young ones over there."

They talked on and on. It seemed no time at all until they were home.

Harry was there, and his wife and the baby. Verna was charmed. She didn't know a home could be like this. Her heart ached for her own hard, cold family. What would become of them?

They all gathered around the hearth and talked until midnight. Their thoughts were mostly with Bill. Sam turned on the radio for the late news. It sobered them. War seemed imminent. Would Bill even get back before it broke?

They waited and prayed. Each day brought fresh news of space flights and missiles a-preparing. Scientists outdid themselves with new discoveries and developments. Russia and the west exchanged more and bitter words.

The day before Christmas, a letter came for Verna, forwarded by the college. She and Sam were just going out for a drive. She slipped it into her pocket.

"I know a place that is like our rock at college," he told her. "Wanna go?"

She nodded. Anything that Sam did was just right with her. On a hillside, a magnificent panorama lay flung out before them. They sat still awhile enjoying it.

Then Verna remembered her letter and took it out.

"I'm almost afraid to open this," she said sadly. She told him something of what had passed at home.

"That's hard for me to understand," he said wonderingly. "But I knew when I first saw you that you hadn't had an easy life. There's something about you — something like — " he paused to find the word he wanted — "like steel in you, only it's beautiful, amber-colored steel." He laughed. "I guess you think I have crazy ideas." He looked sheepish.

"I think you have wonderful ideas," she said softly. A moment of embarrassment crept upon them.

"Open your letter," he said. "You might as well find out what the score is."

There was only one thin sheet in it. She drew it out. It was a bill for her mother's funeral expenses.

She stared at it in horror. Then she gave a cry like a wounded doe and flung her head on Sam's shoulder. He held her close. A long time she clung to him and shook with sobs. He stroked her beautiful amber hair, remembering how often he had wanted to do it. He laid his lips on its softness.

"I'm sorry," she murmured at last, her face still buried in his coat. "I didn't mean to be such a baby."

"You're not a baby," he said. "I don't know anyone who could take that. You're wonderful, VeeEm. Do you know that I love you?"

She stirred in his arms and looked up at him through her amber tears, unbelievingly.

"You couldn't!"

"Oh, yes, I could, and I do," he smiled. She was about to speak but he laid his lips on hers gently and held her warmly close to him. "And I always will love you, darling."

"You aren't afraid of my square corners?"

He laughed and kissed her again. "You haven't any square corners, VeeEm. They're all worn off!"

She took a deep, deep breath of relief. "Then I guess it's all been worth it," she smiled.

"You've taken an awful beating to wear them off, darling." He smoothed her hair back tenderly from her shining, tear-stained face.

She nodded. "I guess I'm really glad mother is gone. She had a hard life. And she did believe, I'm sure. So I know she's better off. Yes, it's been a beating, all the way through, but I'd go through it all over again for this. I love you so, Sam."

At last they noticed that the sky was growing dark.

229

"I think there's a storm coming," he said. Then he turned to her and smiled. "You like storms, don't you! Well, you've had 'em!"

"Yes, and I guess there are more coming — tomorrow."

"We'll meet them together, VeeEm."

"Yes, that will be wonderful. I never found anyone before like you!"

On the way home Sam switched on the radio. They had all formed the habit of being alert for news.

" . . . and it is quite possible that at any time the atmosphere itself may dissolve. Listen to instructions . . ."

They looked at each other aghast.

"Tomorrow is all but here!" Sam spoke solemnly.

They glanced at the well-kept lawns and quiet bungalows they passed, the lights blinking on here and there. "It doesn't seem possible that people are *still* going on the same as ever. Why don't they wake up?" cried Verna.

Sam shook his head sadly. "I don't know. But I'm sure glad the Lord woke us up before it was too late."

They put the car in the garage just as a terrific gust of wind almost snatched the door out of their hands.

In the living room they heard voices.

"Bill!" They rushed in.

There was Bill, smiling and eager, with a handsome, dark-eyed boy.

"Shalom, David!" Sam grasped his hand. "Meet your new cousin-to-be, boy." He turned to Verna. She gasped, blushed, and came forward shyly.

They all crowded around, laughing and making merry.

"Marrying and giving in marriage," thought Bill, *"until — Tomorrow."*